Why Journalism
Still Matters

Michael Schudson

polity

First published in 2018 by Polity Press

Polity Press
65 Bridge Street
Cambridge CB2 1UR, UK

Polity Press
101 Station Landing
Suite 300
Medford, MA 02155, USA

ISBN-13: 978-1-5095-2804-2
ISBN-13: 978-1-5095-2805-9(pb)

A catalogue record for this book is available from the British Library.

Library of Congress Cataloging-in-Publication Data

Names: Schudson, Michael, author.
Title: Why journalism still matters / Michael Schudson.
Description: Cambridge, UK ; Medford, MA : Polity Press, [2018] | Includes
   bibliographical references and index.
Identifiers: LCCN 2018006737 (print) | LCCN 2018009550 (ebook) |
   ISBN 9781509528080 (Epub) | ISBN 9781509528042 (hardback) |
   ISBN 9781509528059 (pbk.)
Subjects: LCSH: Journalism–United States–History–21st century. |
   Journalism–Objectivity–United States–History–21st century. |
   Journalism–Political aspects–United States–History–21st century. | Fake
   news–United States.
Classification: LCC PN4867.2 (ebook) | LCC PN4867.2 .S38 2018 (print) |
   DDC 071/.3–dc23
LC record available at https://lccn.loc.gov/2018006737

Typeset in 10.5 on 12 pt Sabon
by Toppan Best-set Premedia Limited
Printed and bound in the UK by CPI Group (UK) Ltd, Croydon

For further information on Polity, visit our website: politybooks.com

Contents

Personal Acknowledgments

This book reflects on matters I have pondered for many years – from the largely salutary (but consider chapter 4) professionalization of journalism to the misunderstandings of politics that arise from the overemphasis on the "informed citizen" as the moral ideal for democracy. The book integrates some other topics that I should have pondered more (populism, the place of news in everyday life, what technology does and does not "do" to social experience, and whether the "slowness" of democracy should be recognized as a great virtue or as a problem). The significance of professionalism is an underlying theme throughout, and this goes back in my own writing 40 years, but the topic is more fresh and more urgent today than ever. I have been enabled to reconsider it by teaching for the past decade at a "professional school" – the Columbia Journalism School, and I am grateful to the Journalism School and to Columbia University for having provided me this opportunity.

At the same time that I have become an up-close local, observing journalists and journalism, I have become more engaged as a cosmopolitan in an international community of research and thinking in "journalism studies." I am grateful to my colleagues (especially Todd Gitlin, Richard John, and Andie Tucher) in our Journalism School-centered boutique-style doctoral program in communication, to our remarkable students from around the world, and to our alumni who continue to give guidance and moral support to our current students – and to me.

This book would not exist were it not for the director of Polity Press, John Thompson, whose encouragement over many years has been invaluable. In this case, he believed that this volume could and should stretch beyond providing a handy piece of luggage for collecting and transmitting already published papers; it should propose new ideas, recasts old ones, and articulate what it means to claim that journalism still matters. I am grateful also to the excellent staff at Polity, including copyeditor Sarah Dancy.

Thanks to John, there is new life in this book. It is not the only new life in my life. My two-and-a-half-year-old marriage to Julia Sonnevend is new to me still, full of fine adventures that open me to the world afresh, and with a love that only deepens. That love is now enhanced by Noah Peter Schudson, six miraculous months old. If he is not headline news, I don't know what is.

Acknowledgments

The author and publisher gratefully acknowledge the permission granted to reproduce the copyright material in this book.

Chapter 1 originally appeared as "Fourteen or Fifteen Generations: News as a Cultural Form and Journalism as a Historical Formation," *American Journalism* 30/1 (2013), pp. 29–35. Reproduced with permission of the publisher.

Chapter 2 originally appeared as "Walter Lippman's Ghost: An Interview with Michael Schudson," *Mass Communication & Society* 19/3 (2016), pp. 221–9. Reproduced with permission of the publisher.

Chapter 4 originally appeared as "Autonomy from What?" in Rodney Benson and Eric Neveu, eds., *Bourdieu and the Journalistic Field* (Cambridge: Polity, 2005), pp. 214–23.

Chapter 7 originally appeared as "The Crisis in News: Can You Whistle a Happy Tune?" in Jeffrey C. Alexander, Elizabeth Butler Breese, and Maria Luengo, eds., *The Crisis of Journalism Reconsidered: Democratic Culture, Professional Codes, Digital Future* (New York: Cambridge University Press, 2016), pp. 98–115. Reproduced with permission of the publisher.

Chapter 9 originally appeared as "The Multiple Political Roles of Journalism," in Bruce E. Schulman and Julian E. Zelizer, eds., *Media Nation: The Political History of News in*

Modern America (Philadelphia: University of Pennsylvania Press, 2017), pp. 190–205. Reproduced with permission of the publisher.

Chapter 11 originally appeared as "Second Thoughts: Schudson on Schudson," *Journalism Studies* 18/10 (2017), pp. 1334–42. Reproduced with permission of the publisher. *Journalism Studies* can be found online at https://www.tandfonline.com/loi/rjos20.

Introduction

Does journalism matter? More than ever. But to reach that conclusion requires knowing what it matters *to*. And to make a case for journalism's enduring importance, I must also explain what I mean by "journalism" at a time when its borders are more ill-defined than they have ever been before. There are various journalisms, many of them useful, including explicitly partisan journalism, but the journalism whose importance I will make a case for is what I call professional journalism. Professional journalism has been defined simply and, I think, exactly by media scholar Daniel Hallin as journalism in which reporters are "committed more strongly to the norms of the profession than to political ideas."[1] This is the sort of journalism, more than any other kind of commentary on contemporary affairs, that still matters.

To introduce what seems to me vital about journalism, it may help to look at one small decision in the writing of one news story. Consider the story by reporter Richard Pérez-Peña in the *New York Times* October 19, 2017: "Second Federal Judge Blocks the Third Revision of the Travel Ban." The story focuses on the decision just issued by Theodore Chuang, a federal judge in Maryland. Pérez-Peña puts that decision in context. He explains that Judge Derrick Watson in Hawaii was the first judge to pronounce illegal President Donald Trump's third effort at banning travel to the United States from half a dozen majority Muslim countries. Judge Watson had held that it violates a 1965 federal immigration statute prohibiting discrimination based on national origin and he therefore issued a temporary restraining order. Judge Chuang broadened the grounds for holding up Travel Ban 3, finding it arguably illegal on constitutional as well as statutory grounds, and he granted an injunction for an indefinite period.

Pérez-Peña presents this news in flat, emotionless prose, a first indicator that this is what readers should recognize as professional, "objective" journalism. In a second mark of objectivity, he quotes both a plaintiff in the Maryland case supporting Judge Chuang's decision and a Justice Department spokesman criticizing it – standard "let's hear from both sides" writing.

But then, in the fifth paragraph, appears something that breaks from the straightforward matter-of-fact rendition of what happened with a statement that the judges in Hawaii and Maryland who ruled against the travel ban had been appointed by President Barack Obama. That is a fact. The question is why Pérez-Peña mentions it. Here's the full sentence:

> The district judges, both appointed by President Barack Obama, had ruled against an earlier attempt at a travel ban, as had the federal appellate courts for their regions of the country, and the appeals were consolidated and taken up by the Supreme Court, which allowed some parts of the ban to go into effect, pending consideration of the case.

This 59-word sentence is tedious, it's long-winded, but it lays out the chain of events clearly. But then what are those six words – "both appointed by President Barack Obama" – doing? Why does Pérez-Peña interrupt the chronology to insert this bit of history about how the two judges reached their positions?

"Both appointed by President Barack Obama" gives readers sympathetic to the Trump travel bans an explanation outside of the law for why Judges Watson and Chuang ruled as they did. Pérez-Peña does not claim that the judges were guided by their presumably liberal political preferences rather than by a fair-minded interpretation of the law, but he equips readers to entertain this possibility. He answers a question that some readers might have had in mind. I, for one, had exactly that question in mind: were these judges appointed by Republican or by Democratic presidents? I hoped, given my own wish that the travel bans be struck down and that Republican-leaning as well as Democratic-leaning judges would see in them a violation of First Amendment protections of religious freedom, that the judges had been appointed by Republican George W. Bush.

Pérez-Peña could have told us different relevant facts about the two judges. He could have noted that Judge Watson, a native Hawaiian, was the son of a police officer, the first in his family to attend college, a graduate of Harvard Law School. He could have mentioned that Watson's nomination was confirmed by a Senate vote of 94-0. He could have told us that Judge Chuang was the son of Taiwanese immigrants, another Harvard Law School graduate, and from 2009 to 2014 deputy general counsel of the Department of Homeland Security. But Pérez-Peña made a choice and the choice was to recognize in a polarized political world that readers would likely be more interested to know that President Obama appointed these judges rather than that they had outstanding legal credentials and personal connections to law enforcement or homeland security. In offering some context for Judge Chuang's decision, the story goes beyond the simplest "just the facts" account of events. In offering this context rather than other possible contexts, Pérez-Peña makes a decision about how to frame the story and how to guide readers in understanding it. Pérez-Peña or his editors chose a context that recognizes a polarized political world.

The added six words efficiently state a fact. But that is not all they do. They recognize as any reasonable person must that political orientation is, whether we like it or not, a factor in judicial decisions. And in this case they also offer a subtext – a demonstration of the fair-mindedness of the *New York Times* that President Donald Trump repeatedly accuses of encouraging a "witch hunt" against him and publishing an endless stream of "fake news." Acting in a fair-minded way is exactly what news stories (not editorials) in a leading newspaper should be doing, after all. But there is possible damage to our shared civic discourse in the insinuation that judges ignore the law and follow their political preferences; this is cynical in implicitly informing readers that *only* politics, not institutions, matter. The text of "both appointed by President Barack Obama" is unobjectionable, but the subtext is that judges do the political bidding of the presidents who appoint them. This is sometimes true. It is sometimes false – Franklin Roosevelt is probably still rolling over in his grave for appointing Felix Frankfurter to the Supreme Court, a justice who often lined up against the Court's liberals; Dwight Eisenhower likewise regretted appointing Earl Warren and William J. Brennan to the Supreme Court, as did Richard Nixon, for appointing Harry Blackmun, a life-long Republican, who on the Supreme Court crafted the majority opinion in *Roe v. Wade* establishing the constitutionality of laws making some abortions legal.

Whether or not Pérez-Peña made a wise decision to insert "both appointed by President Barack Obama," I feel confident that he wrote not as a political liberal or a political conservative. He wrote as a professional journalist. This is the professionalism that President Donald Trump and others on the right now dismiss as fake, although it is important to note that many on the left have made similar charges over the years against the mainstream media, arguing that they are centrist or even center-right in their implicit view of the world, marginalizing legitimate views on the left.

About the so-called "liberal media": Who in the US presidential elections of 2016 complained the loudest about the bias of the mainstream media? Donald Trump takes the gold medal. But the silver medal would likely go to Bernie Sanders and his supporters. If critics from the Sanders and Trump camps would only pool their rhetorical resources, they would have a case that there is an anti-populist bias in the leading national press.[2] Margaret Canovan, a British political theorist writing in the 1990s, observed that populist movements typically have charismatic leaders "who can make politics personal and immediate instead of being remote and bureaucratic." Amateurism and lack of political experience then become "recommendations." She wrote that the degree of personal power that populist leaders attain is "hard to reconcile with democratic aspirations." At the same time, she suggested, democracies need and sometimes get in populism an "upsurge of faith as a means of renewal."[3] I do not doubt that populism may provide a bracing shot of emotional color into institutional grayness, but it is no substitute for and can be a threat to the integrity of the institutions that sustain democracy.

And this – democracy – is what journalism matters to. Journalism is among the institutions necessary for sustaining democracy, specifically, journalism empowered by legally protected freedom of the press and enabled by sufficient economic support to pursue the news coverage that matters to democracy. The commercial backbone of journalism, especially in the United States, has been undermined by the capabilities of the internet (see chapter 7) but old line news organizations have shown a capacity to produce great journalism even with the cost savings of staff reductions, while some online-only news organizations, often supported by philanthropic contributions and other business model innovations, have also done outstanding energetic and original reporting. In part thanks to the very internet that contributed to the economic crisis of newspaper-centered news organizations, professional news organizations have been able to produce journalism as good or better than ever with leaner staffs.

We should not get too high-minded in talking about journalism. Journalism does many things that are not closely connected to democracy, if connected at all. For instance, it provides bits and pieces of novelty that fit into odd moments of a person's day and it has been doing that for a long time, certainly as far back as 1945 when Bernard Berelson documented during a New York newspaper strike that readers did not miss following any particular story or topic so much as they missed the time-filling enjoyment that news offers. What is new now, as people check and recheck their smartphones throughout the day, is only the frequency and the brevity of these moments.[4] What was a ritual – the newspaper with breakfast, the television news at the dinner hour, radio news in the car – has become a persistent itch that needs to be recurrently scratched.

Journalism, past and present, also provides a location for advertising and therefore presumably a stimulus to economic activity. In addition, journalism is both itself entertainment and a source of information about entertainment – the coverage of sports, books, music, theater. Journalism gives people information about the weather, about automobile traffic, and other topics from new fashions to new technologies to medical breakthroughs that matter to people more on a day to day basis than news of politics.

Where there is not democracy, there is still journalism. Even so, in non-democracies journalists may be waiting for democracy, hoping to be freed to write as conscience dictates, not as party functionaries insist. Journalists as a species, whether working in democracies or in autocratic states, aspire to independent reporting and commentary on current affairs. Reporters in autocratic states may have to work within the constraints imposed by their governments, but they tend to look with real longing toward the greater range of motion that journalists count on in democracies. In contrast, I do not know of any reporters in democracies who yearn to become state propagandists. I know of none who thirst to trade in their substantial level of freedom for immobilizing fetters. Of course, some will barter independence for access, fawning and flattering power despite themselves. But I think they know, somewhere in their hearts, that this violates or threatens to violate the deep strength of their vocation.

Journalism may exist without democracy, but can democracy exist without journalism? Not, I think, in the contemporary world. Journalism grows only more important as an institution of organized skepticism that is central to democratic governance today. As I argue in Chapter 10, one of the key features of representative democracies is not that they empower the people directly to elect their governors, but that they enjoin citizens to be skeptical of the people they have elected. The question of journalism's role in democracy today is befuddled by the vagueness of what the term "journalism" refers to, and that only grows more fuzzy and more contested in the digital age. The line between reporter and bystander blurs when every bystander equipped with a smartphone can send a photograph or a text message instantly to networks that span the globe. The line dividing reporters from advertisers, once fiercely maintained at self-respecting news organizations, has been redrawn to permit so-called "native advertising" that masquerades as news with the full cooperation of the news organizations. And the line between reporting and marketing has blurred when reporters are enjoined by their employers to promote their news stories by posts on social media that simplify, sensationalize, or personalize in messages what they had written in standard professional fashion.

Meanwhile, "democracy" has become too often a largely ceremonial term for journalists and politicians alike, piously invoked but not properly understood. To think usefully about how journalism relates or should relate to democracy, we must consider what sense of these terms we have in mind. With "democracy," the problem is, as we see more and more, and as Fareed Zakaria named it in 1997, that at a time of resurgent "illiberal democracy" around the world, it is urgent to recognize that "democracy" has long been a misleading shorthand for the longer, more awkward and mysterious phrase, "liberal democracy."[5] "Liberal democracy" refers not to democracy that political liberals favor any more than political conservatives do; it refers to a popular election-centered form of government with protections for individual liberties baked into the constitution, into the legal order, and into deep expectations and customs that even electoral majorities are not permitted to revoke. Liberal democracy is not simply a system of competitive elections – after all, a system of competitive elections brought Adolph Hitler to power. It is a system for limiting the capacity of governments – even governments elected by majorities in competitive elections, to trample on the rights of individuals and groups who are not part of those majorities. Until journalists recognize they should not be allegiant to "democracy" shorn of the "liberal" modifier, they cannot understand what their work has to do with democratic ideals.

For me, the sourcebook for thinking through journalism's democratic role remains Walter Lippmann's *Public Opinion*, published in 1922. At different times, different observations made there by Lippmann leap out as cautions for us a century later. I call attention to one of these in Chapter 2, where, in my fanciful reading of what Lippmann's ghost might want to tell us, the ghost notes *Public Opinion*'s much quoted remark that journalism "is like the beam of a searchlight that moves restlessly about, bringing one episode and then another out of darkness into vision," but he then urges attention to the sentence that immediately precedes that famous one: "The press is no substitute for institutions."[6] In the context of 2017 and 2018 and Donald Trump's United States – with parallel concerns in Brexit-era Britain, Viktor Orbán's Hungary, Recep

Tayyip Erdoğan's Turkey, Benjamin Netanyahu's Israel, Vladimir Putin's Russia, and resurgent extreme right-wing thrusts toward political power in Germany, Denmark, the Netherlands, France, and Austria – it is vital to recognize the importance of institutions. Chief among them are an independent judiciary, the rule of law, a civil service loyal to an oath of office rather than to an incumbent prime minister or president, and an independent press dedicated to verifiable truth and protected by civil liberties enforceable by law.

Among the missing elements of democracy in populist regimes is respect for independent media. A recent study of how left-wing populist presidents in Latin America use Twitter finds in their tweets an obsession with responding to the latest news and an equal obsession with attacking enemies, prominent among them the news media. There seems no tolerance in the outlook of populist leaders for independent thinkers or independent institutions. They live in a Manichean world – if you are not for me, you are against me. All interest is self-interest. All knowledge is only a disguise for power.

For many political theorists, a glory of liberal societies is the space between the state, the market, and the private life of families – at its best, the flourishing of a vibrant associational life or "civil society," but this arena goes entirely unrecognized or, worse, gets vilified by populist leaders. The vilification typically focuses on news organizations, whether profitmaking, state-supported, or philanthropically underwritten. This is not surprising, certainly, but it is no less corrosive for being anticipated. And it is encouraged by a great but nonetheless double-edged development in journalism since the mid-twentieth century – the rise of what I call *Objectivity 2.0*. In Chapter 3, I provide an account of the rise of journalism as a profession in the United States, reaching a stage of self-consciousness in the 1920s with a broad acceptance of what I name *Objectivity 1.0*. In the twenties, as journalists went about their work, they felt themselves struggling to stay afloat in waters infested by the sharks of state propaganda and corporate public relations, all of them trying to bite off pieces of independent journalism for their own purposes. American journalists, in self-defense, settled into routines of verifying facts, of matching a quotation from a Democrat with a quotation from a Republican, a balancing to keep their news from capture by the sharks. And this was the approach that came to maturity and self-confidence in the 1950s.

But then, in the late 1960s and 1970s, Objectivity 2.0 was overlaid atop of Objectivity 1.0, without erasing it. News à la Objectivity 2.0 became more probing and more analytical, sketching in a context for understanding events and not just a flat account of what happened yesterday. This greater emphasis on interpretation in reporting was sometimes justified in the newspaper world as a necessary move to give readers something they could not get from television, but it was much more than economics. It was part of a powerful cultural shift. Objectivity 2.0 news was not only more enterprising and investigative, not only more analytical, but more negative. From the 1960s to the 1990s, journalism became more and more critical of presidential candidates – and, let me underline this, increasingly negative about presidential candidates of *both* parties. Thomas Patterson's analysis of *Time* and *Newsweek* reporting found 75 percent of "evaluative references" to presidential candidates John F. Kennedy and Richard Nixon were positive in 1960, but in the next 32 years they became much more negative and never again reached anything close to that 75 percent figure; in 1992 only 40 percent of evaluations of Bill Clinton and George Bush were positive.[7] This was part of a move to hold power – left and right – to account, what former *Washington Post* executive editor Leonard Downie, Jr. and his *Washington Post* colleague Robert Kaiser have called "accountability journalism."[8]

Pérez-Peña's story on the Trump travel ban is largely written in a sophisticated version of Objectivity 1.0, but "both appointed by President Barack Obama" is a phrase that uses a fact to incorporate interpretation – not necessarily Pérez-Peña's interpretation, but evoking for readers a possible interpretation they may or may not have considered. It is a subtle move. It takes the story into an Objectivity 2.0 mode where the reporter is well aware that news stories require contexts to be understandable. Sketching in context is a part of the reporter's job where choices must be made and judgment must be exercised and there is no single best way to do this. But professionals at least have the training, the experience, and the social support of a newsroom to do it better than most amateurs could do with the same materials.

Journalists must make judgments. The task to which they devote themselves is to do that well. They recognize, at least intermittently, the pitfalls in their paths. Journalists – along with civics teachers, reformers, scholars, and patriotic orators – are less likely to recognize that they should not accept that journalism's larger objective is to enable and enhance democracy if, by democracy, they mean only majority rule in contested elections. The American founders did not seek democracy in this sense (they actually worked to avoid it). The US Constitution is not a text for democracy in this sense, either. (For a brief overview of the changing ideals of citizenship and democracy in US history, see Chapter 8.) And journalists today should have no truck with democracy when it is shorn of its "liberal" modifier. They should instead embrace "liberal democracy." For the sake of liberty, the protection of minorities, and the advancement of a decent society, they should help us relearn these civic values.

Not all of the essays gathered here are fully cognizant of this. Only the most recent of the essays, for obvious reasons, recognize that what has been a problem for some years or decades in Hungary, Turkey, Russia, and elsewhere has become an American problem too. Mr. Trump's electoral triumph for the US, like the Brexit vote for Britain, has been enormously clarifying on this point. From now on, even if Donald Trump should be removed from office through impeachment proceedings or should fail to be reelected, it is clear that Americans are not immune to vulgar breeds of illiberalism.

What "Liberal" Means in "Liberal Democracy"

A liberal democracy is *democratic* if it empowers the general public to exercise a primary role in selecting the individuals who will hold public office, doing so through a political system that permits two or more political parties and that equips the public and its parties with the freedom of speech and association to compete for office. A liberal democracy is *liberal* if it empowers the elected leadership only within the boundaries of recognizing citizens' civil and political rights, honoring the institutional divisions of governmental power that assure the protection of those rights, and working within the rule of law to protect both institutions and individuals even when doing so violates the electoral judgment of the people.

Journalists seeking to help build a good society through their work should understand these definitional requirements of liberal democracy. They should regularly remind their audiences that in liberal democracy people through elections entrust leaders with great authority, but it is an authority delimited and confined. The news media should of course recognize the legitimacy of elected officials and the officials they appoint, and treat them with respect accordingly, but at the same time they should grant them only the most provisional trust. Leaders in democracies are elected not to do their will, but to do their job.

Democratic leaders can be held to their rightful task only in societies where there is a healthy web of accountability – a set of quasi-independent institutions of audit and review inside government, a set of independent institutions in civil society dedicated to the review and critique of power and often prepared to go to court in defense of and in advancement of their findings of criminal or negligent acts by elected officials, and news organizations with the power, authority, professionalism, and persistence to make public the shortcomings of those who govern.

I think most Americans – and certainly most American journalists looking at Washington today – feel as bewildered as Hillary Rodham Clinton about "what happened" in the 2016 election. We thought we knew this country reasonably well, but awakened to a realization of how limited our understanding has been. Our brains are beset, our stomachs unsettled, we cannot digest what we have to constitutionally swallow – even as knowledge accumulates that this election was in some measure tainted, if not stolen, by Russian interference – interference that, at this writing, seems to have been welcomed and encouraged by Trump campaign officials, including Donald Trump, Jr., at a Trump Tower meeting with a Russian who promised to provide incriminating information about Democratic presidential candidate Hillary Clinton. Two days after that meeting, Donald Jr. had a phone call with his father (with lawyers listening in at both ends of the call) that he is unwilling to discuss before congressional investigators. The question, of course, is what the younger Trump said to his father or, in the language of Watergate, what did the candidate himself know and when did he know it.[9]

Unfortunately, the 2016 US presidential election may end up in the history books marked by an asterisk.

We can see, in retrospect, that liberal opinion has contributed a great deal to this massive failure of American democratic practice. Think of the pious and platitudinous endorsement of popular sentiment to be found as much on the left as on the right. "Power to the people" was a leading slogan of the student left in the 1960s. But there is little to praise about the rule of simple majorities if they proceed by illiberalism – reckless trashing of the news media, xenophobia, racism, disregard for constitutional protections, contempt for decisions of duly elected or appointed judges conscientiously pursuing their work, and so forth. Where in popularly advertised liberalism can you find a rhetorical emphasis that liberal democracy is not "majority rule"? Advocacy of "deliberative democracy" or "participatory democracy" helped to create new participatory forms, some of them quite useful. But these reforms, like any others, should be judged not by the purity of motives behind them but by their performance in practice. I concede the purity of motive of many people who have advocated more participatory democratic institutions or more transparency in governmental processes. But as soon as "participation" and "transparency" became unassailable slogans, we should have recognized that something must be very wrong with them and we should have gone on high alert to protect the integrity of democratic institutions from plebiscitarian mania.

There is a difference between participatory democracy and majority rule, on the one hand, and accountable democracy and constitutional rule, on the other. Liberals have been too ready to attack experts and the very idea that there is such a thing as expertise – and I insist in several of the essays in these pages that journalism, when it is dedicated to the professional values that have become central to it over the past century, offers a model of expertise that is far from perfect but has proven itself in practice. That knowledge is a veil for power is as much a reflex on the left as on the right and it is likewise to be faulted. The intellectual challenge is not to brashly pronounce that nonpartisanship is a fraud and knowledge but a thin disguise for power (but how could we know that – if all knowledge is fraudulent, what authorizes our own pronouncement that all knowledge is fraudulent?). The task is, instead, to come to understand what the limitations to human constructions of knowledge are. and how, over time, some systems have repeatedly proved themselves reliable and others have fallen by the wayside. We can agree at the outset with the skeptics and the cynics that there is no perfect system of fact-gathering and fact-interpretation. We begin there, but we do not end there.

In the Columbia Journalism School where I teach as a kind of sociologist-historian in residence, I think there are two sacred words. One is "report." Your job is to seek the truth through "reporting." Do a "deeply reported" piece. "Report against your own assumptions" – that is, make sure you explore positions and lines of inquiry that others might hold who do not share your own preconceptions. This is the tone of Objectivity 1.0. It is still vital.

The other key word, equally sacred in Pulitzer Hall, is "story." You have to know enough context and background for your assignment and enough about where it fits in the wider world to construct the skeleton on which the factual flesh of the piece can hang.

The language of report and the language of story circulate in journalism schools and in newsrooms without much concern about the inevitable tension between them – the language of reporting asks journalists to completely withhold judgment, but the language of "story" requires choice, selection, judgment. This need not be and should not be personal judgment or partisan judgment, but professional judgment. My claim about this is simple: there is such a thing in journalism. There is such a thing as professionalism among journalists – not all journalists, but among those who pride themselves on evidence-based reporting, on following the facts wherever they may lead, and, whatever their personal political views might be, on following the "story" wherever it may lead and whomever it may offend. Objectivity 2.0 did not erase that commitment but it does complicate it. Interpretation becomes more necessary and more visible and, as news becomes more interpretive, judgment becomes more present and the need to defend it more omnipresent.

None of us can escape our own standpoint, but most of us at some point try to. For instance, we know that out of loyalty and hope, we overestimate the chances that our favorite team will win the big game this weekend. But if we are betting on the game, if we are betting real money, we are usually capable of discounting for the bias we know we possess. We may dismiss the professionalism of doctors and say that, generally speaking, doctors overprescribe and over-recommend expensive surgery to make money, not to practice medicine, but in an emergency we put our trust in their hands, not our own or those of a spouse or a drinking buddy. However much we may emphasize the shortcomings of modern medicine in the abstract, in an emergency most people let the experts overrule their own instincts and preferences.

To take a different kind of example, when a student seeks advice of a teacher, a child seeks advice from a parent, or a friend seeks advice from a friend, the teacher, the parent, and the friend may say, "I can't tell you what to do, but if I were in your shoes...." The thought-experiment of "if I were in your shoes" is precisely an effort to step outside one's own standpoint. Some people do this better than others and, in your circle, you know who they are just as I do in my circle, and we seek people's advice accordingly.

In journalism, professionalism is the effort to step outside a personal or political standpoint and into a professional mission. And the professional mission is to follow the story rather than following political or other preferences. The failure of mainstream professionalism is not that it puts politics above the story – the professional always puts the story first. But the professional journalist does not recognize all phenomena as part of a story and may not see a story that does not shout "story!" against the background of unconscious assumptions among journalists, their colleagues, co-workers, friends, family, and neighbors. In this respect, as I argue in Chapter 4, there is a danger in the so-called mainstream media that they take some unstated assumptions about "what reasonable people think" for granted and they may thereby manifest a smugness that excludes some perfectly reasonable people from the circle that the journalists accept as reasoned.

Following the story may be uncomfortable for journalists with strong partisan leanings because the story may unearth unpleasant truths about favored policies or persons. Where did the story arise that Hillary Clinton used a private email server for official State Department business, some of it highly confidential, when she was Secretary of State? From work done by reporters for the *New York Times*. And where did the public learn of the multiple charges of sexual harassment in the workplace against Harvey Weinstein, a key Democratic Party donor? The *New York Times* and *The New Yorker*. I do not doubt that most reporters at the *New York Times* tend to have liberal sympathies. What I doubt is that they give them free rein. And if they believe that "both appointed by President Barack Obama" is a centrally relevant piece of information in a highly politicized era, it goes in the story; and if that alarms some readers who think this offers up a cynical theory of how the judges arrived at their decisions, so be it.

Does professional journalism still have a place in a world where so much communication is online and so much of that communication is on social media, where it is hard for people to keep in mind where their information comes from? A friend? A friend of a friend? A conventional newspaper or television or radio station in its online incarnation? Or any number of outrageous efforts at disinformation and misinformation that also circulate online? Does the relative hegemony of professional news organizations disappear?

That would be a serious misreading, whether in the wishful thinking of Donald Trump or in the libertarian or democratic utopianism of enthusiasts that the internet offers a self-correcting wisdom-of-crowds substitute for professionalism and expertise. My reasoning here is very simple. What news items have the president or the Congress, governors or mayors, or corporate executives been forced by law or by public opinion to respond to? There is an uncountable amount of talk online, from email to Facebook to Twitter to comments readers write to websites, reviews they post on TripAdvisor, active strings of comments about pregnancy and infancy posted on "What to Expect When You're Expecting." On the whole, this explosion of communications seems to me to offer astonishing benefits in terms of the circulation of medical information, advice to the lovelorn, information about a place you may want to visit, information about how to reach people who share the same rare disease you have, and so on. But in this galaxy of information, how much of what is produced by nonprofessional journalists leads powerful individuals and institutions to respond?

Little or none, I suspect. In contrast, *Washington Post* reporting helped end the brief career of Michael Flynn as White House national security advisor; the *New Yorker* was instrumental in providing facts that quickly destroyed the brief career of Anthony Scaramucci as White House communications director; and *Politico*, a largely online political reporting news organization begun in 2007 and now boasting 500 employees, brought down Health and Human Services Secretary Tom Price with their investigative reporting that documented Mr. Price had traveled regularly on privately chartered jets, charging $400,000 to the federal government. In a later story, *Politico* reporters found that Dr. Brenda Fitzgerald, the director of the Centers for Disease Control, the enormously important federal health agency that plays a key role in campaigns against cigarette smoking, was trading in tobacco company stocks – she resigned within 24 hours. And London's *Daily Mail* reported that both the ex-wives of White House staff secretary Rob Porter had accused him of verbal and physical abuse; while denying the allegations, Porter resigned his position the next day.[10] In each case, facts secured by professional journalists, at old line or at online news organizations, had consequences.

Remember those names – Flynn, Scaramucci, Price, Fitzgerald, Porter – brought down by professional journalists because they had gathered credible information that was seriously damaging to the reputations of these highly placed government officials. And this leaves aside the extraordinary case of Hollywood powerhouse Harvey Weinstein, whose many years of sexual exploitation of women in his employ or seeking to work for him was exposed by the *New York Times* and the *New Yorker*, touching off the #metoo movement in the United States and soon thereafter around the world. In this effort, professional news organizations continue to play a vital role. The #metoo movement has spread from Hollywood to the sexual exploitation of subordinates in the restaurant business, colleges and universities, the classical music world, architecture, and news media organizations themselves.

How often have the White House or other power centers been forced to respond to nonprofessional efforts at news? This is a question that I have not yet researched but I do have a hypothesis: at least for the American case, the powerful are scarcely ever called to account by nonprofessional communications. WikiLeaks may be the exception that proves the rule. Julian Assange, its founder and director, was not a partisan political figure but a crusader against all power, it seems, an anarchist by word and deed, and certainly not a professional journalist. But even Assange, for all of his eye-catching celebrity, found his greatest traction when he cooperated with and published through mainstream professional news organizations in multiple countries.

One of the troubles for the news media is, as Lippmann put it in 1922, that democracies "act without a reliable picture of the world, that governments, schools, newspapers and churches make such small headway against the more obvious failings of democracy, against violent prejudice, apathy, preference for the curious trivial as against the dull important, and the hunger for sideshows and three-legged calves."[11]

I have very little to say in the pages that follow about the taste for sideshows and three-legged calves. We have collectively not worried enough about sideshows, even to the point of electing in the United States a sideshow barker as president, someone who takes the presidency to be no more deserving of respect, no more requiring of a certain degree of subordinating one's own ego to the traditions and dignity of office, than would be in the case of, say, selling real estate or running a TV show. And of course it is not only the popular taste for sideshows – it is equally the taste of news organizations that cater to the popular taste. And now a taste for sideshows is also to be found in even the most august news organizations, including the *New York Times* and the *Washington Post*, that encourage – essentially require – their reporters to push their stories out on social media and to appear to the public (on social media) in the garb of the social media pundit, able to quip and carp and tease and snarl and joke with the best of them in an effort to promote whatever their latest story may happen to be.

Do news organizations surrender to the tastes of audiences or bow to what they suspect are the tastes of audiences, out of the search for profits? Or do they protect their reporters and editors from offering only what might be today's equivalent of the three-legged calf – perhaps a pope who endorsed Donald Trump for president or a Hillary Clinton-coordinated child sexual abuse ring operating out of a pizza parlor. "News" has always thrived on the taste for sideshows that, to different degrees, we all share. Journalists do not want simply to inform, like dutiful and uninspired school teachers; they want to astonish. There seems always to be something odd, unbelievable, or bizarre that turns out to be absolutely true. And well before the internet journalists sought to evoke in their readers "astonishment, not understanding."[12] News stories that produce astonishment are much easier to "like" and to "like" and to "link to" than the latest comprehensive analysis of the latest tax bill before the Congress or the Parliament. We have long used "news" for conversational gambits; tax reform is not a conversation starter.

To respond, as Walter Lippmann did in 1920, in his book *Liberty and the News*, with a call for higher standards in journalism, for independent think-tanks (what Lippmann referred to as "political observatories"), university research, and schools of journalism, might seem to many, he admitted, "a gray business in a vivid world." And yet, Lippmann continued, "I am convinced that we shall accomplish more by fighting for truth than by fighting for our theories. It is a better loyalty. It is a humbler one, but it is also more irresistible." He concluded: "The administration of public information toward greater accuracy and more successful analysis is the highway of liberty."[13]

The essays collected in this volume – with five of them published here for the first time – try to focus on that highway, a road that is vital to liberal democracies. Journalism is not alone in traveling that road and, indeed, less alone than ever before. Civil society is richer than ever, university research more extensive than ever. Individual citizens who volunteer their untutored but often very real expertise in editing Wikipedia entries or in starting their own blogs are important, too. So are governmental institutions like "inspectors-general" and other internal auditing agencies that report not only to the government but to the public. Greater accuracy and more successful analysis is the business all of these travelers who, together, comprise a web of accountability for holding power in check. And professional journalism? It has become more and more necessary to democracy as the common forum for many disparate and disconnected institutions that make up this web. Professional journalism is the commons where public attention, public monitoring, and even public participation in governance takes place, not only at elections but year-round. It is a "keystone" institution because it is through the news that the public learns of the work of all the other accountability institutions – from the litigation undertaken by various advocacy organizations in civil society to the audits of government agencies conducted by government inspectors-general. It is through what appears in the news media and particularly in the news outlets with prestige and presence in Washington and in state capitals that government leaders are forced to respond.

Without this service that journalism provides, the practice of liberal democracy as a form of government intrinsically committed to holding in check the power of elected leaders would not be impossible, but it would be substantially more difficult. Executive power is limited through the division of authority among branches of government and by the division of power between state or provincial governments and national or federal government, and by the limitations of even the most powerful officials imposed on them by constitutional restraints. But all of this requires that elected leaders who may be seeking to usurp their legitimate authority be held publicly accountable so that they can be popularly punished by the voters at the next election.

Various forms of journalism, including partisan journalism, can contribute to this effort. But in the long run, for the public to be swayed from positions people have already staked out, and for government officials to respond to charges that they have behaved corruptly or unconstitutionally or simply rashly and unwisely, the source of information has to come from organizations that hold themselves to the highest standards of verification, fact-checking, independence, and original research – and, if the journalists learn that they got it wrong, that they make corrections prominently and quickly. That is exactly the aspiration of professional journalism. And it is an aspiration achieved much more by trained journalists who seek to achieve it than by untrained amateurs who do not.

Part I
Where Journalism Came From

1

14 or 15 Generations: News as a Cultural Form and Journalism as a Historical Formation

This chapter was originally a presentation at an annual meeting of the Association for Education in Journalism and Mass Communication, and was later published in *American Journalism* in 2013.

A perennial issue for historians is to determine for the topic at hand the relative importance of change and continuity and where on the calendar to locate turning points or times of transition.

Different thinkers take different positions on these matters, but professional historians typically are more interested to focus on and seek to explain change than continuity.

In contrast, Bill Kovach and Tom Rosenstiel, distinguished journalists, eloquent interpreters of American journalism, and leaders in their profession, emphasize continuity in the history of American journalism. They stake this claim in their influential book *The Elements of Journalism*. They begin by associating themselves with media scholar Jim Carey's view that, as they paraphrase it, holds that "in the end journalism simply means carrying on and amplifying the conversation of people themselves."[1] There is an abiding and somehow comforting element of truth in this. But Kovach and Rosenstiel then add that this definition has "held so consistent through history, and proven so deeply ingrained in the thinking of those who produce news through the ages, that it is in little doubt."[2] In fact, they continue, "the basic standards of newsworthiness have varied very little throughout history."

That is the assertion I dispute here. They go on to approvingly quote journalist and journalism scholar Mitchell Stephens's generalization:

> The basic topics with which... news accounts have been concerned, and the basic standards by which they evaluate newsworthiness, seem to have varied very little. Humans have exchanged a similar mix of news with a consistency throughout history and cultures that makes interest in this news seem inevitable, if not innate.[3]

If this is right, there is nothing new under the sun – nothing, at any rate, of much import, nothing that touches on journalism's fundamentals.

But it isn't right. If you look back at the *Pennsylvania Gazette* published by Benjamin Franklin in the 1700s, you see that, like the very few other papers of the day, it printed largely foreign news (more than 90 percent according to the most thorough study we have, with only 6 percent concerning Philadelphia and Pennsylvania).[4] There was scarcely anything in Franklin's pages reflective of the local conversation. In France, newspapers that circulated in the countryside focused on "national or universal themes over local, specific ones." Local papers that focused on local news became common only from the 1870s.[5] In India, local news became a staple of newspapers only since the early 1970s. Before then, as one well-informed observer has put it, Indians had "not yet come to look upon the press as something of intimate relation to themselves."[6] This is perhaps an unusual case, since the Indian press was not even written in any of the languages most Indians spoke – hard to carry on the conversation of the people themselves if you don't speak the language! But, in many countries, newspapers and even broadcasting did not in the beginning aspire to, let alone practice, a journalism that took the tastes and interests of the people themselves into consideration.

Consider whether it is "consistent throughout history," as Kovach and Rosenstiel say, or "throughout history and cultures," as Stephens puts it, that journalists report on the so-called private lives of public figures. A presidential candidate's extramarital affair in 1940 would have been of great interest to many people, I suspect, but it was not news as far as journalists were concerned. Reporters knew very well that Republican candidate Wendell Willkie was having an affair with the *New York Herald Tribune*'s book review editor Irita van Doren.[7] None of them wrote about it. But Gary Hart's affair was big news when he sought the Democratic nomination for president in 1988. What explains this change?

This is the sort of thing historians are typically interested in – "change over time." A Universal and Eternal Constant is necessarily silent about change. Why, then, are Kovach and Rosenstiel so interested in reaching for the timeless and the universal in journalism? They go pretty far in this direction, positing that "people crave news out of basic instinct, what we call the Awareness Instinct." People need to know the unknown and they use news for practical purposes. News responds to the human need to be aware of one's environment. People "need to know what is going on over the next hill, to be aware of events beyond their direct experience. Knowledge of the unknown gives them security; it allows them to plan and negotiate their lives. Exchanging this information becomes the basis for creating community, making human connections."[8]

They have something here. After all, it does feel like there's something relatively timeless and relatively universal at least in the gossipy side of news. If journalism were true to the interests of the public, and not busy repressing information for the sake of some precepts about the dignity of our political life, Wendell Willkie's adultery would have been widely discussed in the press, just as Gary Hart's was half a century later. Perhaps this is what Kovach and Rosenstiel have in mind. But if that's the case, it is all the more interesting and worthy of remark – and research – that other forces overcame gut-level instinct for generations of journalists. Why should that have been so? Why should newspapers seeking profits have adopted norms of reporting that flew in the face of attracting readers and serving the Awareness Instinct? To give Kovach and Rosenstiel the benefit of the doubt, can we say that there are some constants about journalism somewhere? That journalism – at least if given free rein (which, of course, it never is) – would invariably provide a lot of the same stuff that seems to always and everywhere draw popular attention?

Stuff about assault and murder, sex and romance, conflict and competition, mystery and wonder, birth and death, health and illness, babies left on doorsteps – and perhaps any juicy bits about kings, queens, presidents, and prime ministers? Would these stories – were a perfect journalistic world to be unrestrained by politics, culture, intellectual pretension, professional pride, party loyalty, and religious preoccupation – flow unceasingly throughout journalism history?

Maybe. Maybe not. Maybe the reality is even less flattering to the human species. Consider the observation of the anthropologist Claude Lévi-Strauss on the origins of writing. The one thing that has invariably accompanied the emergence of writing, he says, is:

> the exploitation ... of mankind. This exploitation made it possible to assemble workpeople by the thousand and set them tasks that taxed them to the limits of their strength ... the primary function of writing, as a means to communication, is to facilitate the enslavement of other human beings. The use of writing for disinterested ends, and with a view to satisfactions of the mind in the fields either of science or the arts, is a secondary result of its invention – and may even be no more than a way of reinforcing, justifying, or dissimulating its primary function.[9]

But Lévi-Strauss's claim to a universal and timeless truth about writing is as unsatisfying as Kovach and Rosenstiel's that journalism expresses and responds to an Awareness Instinct. In both cases, the authors stand at a huge distance from what they are trying to fathom. The relative changelessness they see in media history takes a perspective that seems fit for understanding the slow shifting of a coastline or the barely perceptible aging of a mountain range, a geological sense of time ill-suited to understanding activities where changes in years, decades, and centuries matter deeply to us. Let me offer an alternative framework for media history, alternative to this quest for the universal. Let me propose we think of news as a cultural form – like the novel, the scientific experiment, or the sonata – something that is produced through a set of activities and conventions and practices, often by a person or group of people specifically organized for that purpose. People have always eaten – now, there's an activity that responds to a basic instinct. But settled agriculture, as a specific set of practices and activities by groups of people who organize their time and lives to produce edible food, is by no means timeless. It begins with the "agricultural revolution" 10,000 years ago. The history of news as a separate, identifiable, and ongoing activity does not go back beyond the 1500s in the West; the regular, periodical publication in organs whose main purpose is the general circulation (as opposed to circulation among a specialized group of merchants or government officials) of information about public occurrences both foreign and domestic does not go back beyond the 1600s. Even then, news organs had little to do with constituting a public life; they were a significant part of an informational structure sustaining a commercial world. Insofar as what we mean by journalism today relates to the constitution of a public life, an institution in which criticism and discussion is part of its function, there is little one could call journalism until there is something amounting to a so-called public sphere, which is to say, until the eighteenth century.

If "news" or "journalism" requires a general audience, it does not appear until some time in the 1600s and then only incompletely; if it requires a safe haven for dissenting opinion within a public sphere, it does not arise until the 1700s and then only in a very few places. If it requires hiring reporters rather than printing any document or stray tidbit that walks in the door, then there is little to be called journalism until the 1800s. Media historians have a task of understanding why this novel creature – the periodical publication of reports on current affairs for general readers – arose where it did (and not elsewhere) and when it did (and not earlier, or later).

To advertise my claim another way, journalism is modern – that is, it originated not before the 1600s, and it has developed worldwide as a product not of independent invention but of European colonial expansion. To a surprising extent its global spread has been particularly influenced by American innovations; the spread of US influence on other journalisms goes back far before CNN to the nineteenth century. This is another story, but American journalists invented and disseminated internationally the practice of interviewing. American journalists in the period 1880 to 1920, as two separate studies by both British and Dutch scholars show, originated the essential elements of a modern transnational news discourse and news form.[10] It may be that Kovach and Rosenstiel are really doing a kind of philosophy of journalism, one that seeks some kind of ontological essence, but they have phrased their quest in historical terms, where they should be – by my understanding of history, at any rate – examining the various social forces that have shaped news and prompted changes in its construction, delivery, and influence over time and likewise led to sometimes notably different formations of journalism across different nations.

Before modernity as well as since, people gossiped. In both premodern and modern times, people have asked travelers what they saw and heard elsewhere. But it will not do to say we have journalism because people have always wanted to know things and talk about them any more than we have sonatas because the hills are alive with the sound of music. We do not have controlled experiments because people have always been curious about the natural world. An Awareness Instinct does not explain journalism – or science – any more than a Sonata Instinct explains sonatas. News stories, like sonatas and controlled experiments, are specifically modern cultural forms. And the newspaper, as the first regularly published and generally distributed publicly available vehicle for news, was a cultural form of special significance to democracy because it was through the newspaper and in the newspaper that a distinctively modern construction called "the public sphere" came into being.

Journalism, as we have come to think of it and as we have come to value it over the past two centuries, partakes of and has been shaped by the spirit of the Enlightenment. The Enlightenment held a heady and overconfident view that permanent solutions to all problems of knowledge could be achieved through objective methods and rational procedures.[11] As historian Isaiah Berlin explains, the Enlightenment proclaimed "the autonomy of reason and the methods of the natural sciences, based on observation as the sole reliable method of knowledge, and the consequent rejection of the authority of revelation, sacred writings and their accepted interpreters, tradition, prescription, and every form of non-rational and transcendent source of knowledge."[12]

Most of us, these days, if we still cling to Enlightenment ideals, sprinkle them with generous quantities of counter-Enlightenment skepticism, whether drawn from French philosopher and social theorist Michel Foucault or from sociology and anthropology, or from a history of too many failures and disappointments of Enlightenment-inspired projects. And yet I think it is fair to say that journalism – as a particular practice aimed at contributing truths to public discourse, and discussion and criticism in relation to governments – still generally holds to the liberating optimism of Enlightenment aspirations.

The key theorist of media history who takes this Enlightenment transformation of consciousness most seriously is sociologist and philosopher Jürgen Habermas, who sees it as the decisive moment in the emergence of what he calls a "public sphere." He makes two large claims. The first is that at the end of the eighteenth century, that is, at the time of the Enlightenment, people were able for the first time in history to come together as equals to reason critically about public affairs. His second big claim is that this original opening was shut down in the nineteenth century by concentrated capitalist ownership serving its own financial interests rather than the public good. I want to focus on the first claim. The second claim is simply wrong. Habermas, at least in 1962, saw the market as the enemy of the public, when the weight of evidence, in my view, is that the market has been as often the friend as the foe of public good, and even helped construct a more inclusive and participatory public sphere than the Enlightenment provided or imagined.[13]

For Habermas, public opinion was something new in the eighteenth-century world. Before then, there was what we might think of as folklore, what he calls "mere opinion," a "sediment of history" rather than an active force. It is something that is just enduringly there, not something that had to be invented and preserved through "institutional protections." The public sphere, in contrast, developed only in the mid-eighteenth century in urban centers of Western Europe as parliaments gathered some force within monarchies and as social changes, first in literary realms and then in political domains, carved out a space where private people could come together as equals to discuss the politics of the day – without fear of reprisal. They gathered in coffeehouses and other public spaces to talk and argue, basing their discussion on the "informational newspapers" and "critically oriented weeklies."[14]

We take public discussion of political controversy so much for granted that it comes as something of a shock to recognize what Habermas says here – that public discussion, as a normal element in politics, was invented in Europe in the eighteenth century and not before; that the newspaper and the coffeehouse taught people something that over several thousand years they had not already figured out – how to engage in public discussion. The claim is that the eighteenth-century precursors of Starbucks and Fox News (the latter in some ways more like early newspapers than is the *New York Times*) created the modern world of public opinion and political discourse.

I do not expect you to swallow the Habermasian story whole, although I believe that it is largely right. What I want to suggest is that Habermas's view at least recognizes that there have been significant changes in what journalism is, what it stands in relationship to, and what the stakes may be in coming to grips with what historically constituted forms mean and how they matter to us. Journalism is not eternal. It is not universal. There are reasons it developed when and where it did. And in the long history of humankind, it has existed for only 14 or so generations. This had not occurred to me until reading Stuart Firestein's book, *Ignorance: How It Drives Science*. There, in offering a skeptical, but nonetheless loving, account of science from an insider's viewpoint (Firestein is a neurobiologist), he refers to the scientific enterprise as one "that has been continuously pursued through nearly 15 generations. Its worldview is not one that has taken hold in all cultures, and the impetus to see the world as a tractable mystery is not one that is really common."[15]

Journalism – as most of its historians understand it – is an enterprise of roughly the same vintage, and that means some 14 or 15 generations. And in that span of time, there have been various journalisms and major shifts in what is covered and how it is covered and, indeed, whether "covering" or evaluating "newsworthiness" are even tasks with which the printers and publishers of information about current public affairs thought they should be concerned (as opposed to chronicling, advancing a partisan or a theological or a government agenda, or providing a vehicle for miscellaneous contributions). Those differences, and those changes – and their current transformation or unraveling or whatever it is journalism is going through today – belong at the center of journalism history.

2

Walter Lippmann's Ghost: An Interview

Unannounced and generally unreported, the ghost of journalist and public intellectual Walter Lippmann (1889–1974) attended the International Communication Association (ICA) annual conference in Seattle in 2014. Michael Schudson, Columbia Journalism School professor, sociologist, and media scholar, was there and managed to obtain this exclusive interview. It was published originally in 2016 as "Walter Lippmann's Ghost: An Interview with Michael Schudson" in *Mass Communication & Society*. It has been edited slightly to bring it up to date.

Michael: Walter, what a wonderful surprise to see you here in Seattle at the ICA! But I thought you died in 1974!

Walter: You don't believe in ghosts? Well neither did I. And we do not get permission to travel back among civilians very often, but I had heard so much about Microsoft and Starbucks that I just had to. (Besides, over the past few decades I have learned quite a lot about Nirvana.)

Michael: Well, it's just wonderful that you are here. I would love to get your impressions about journalism and democracy these days, particularly in light of the program you hoped journalists would adopt back at the time you wrote *Liberty and the News* (1920) and then *Public Opinion* (1922).[1] So let me begin with the sad fact that the population of journalists in American newspaper newsrooms declined from 67,000 in 1992 to 59,000 in 2002 to roughly 40,000 today. In such a world, is there any hope for getting the kind of news coverage a democracy requires?

Walter: Well, as you are probably aware, a 1971 study found 39,000 journalists in newspapers then, essentially identical to what you have today. Yes, I realize that there are about 50 percent more people in the country than in those days. But thanks to computers, websites, aggregators, brilliant sources of information like Wikipedia or YouTube, stunningly good search engines like Google, and even a newspaper's own past stories online, today's reporters are simply a lot more efficient in researching a story than they used to be. Yes, 20,000 newsroom jobs have been lost since 2002, but how many reporters would you need to rehire to reach the same level of quality that newsrooms offered then? Surely less than 20,000. Is it less than 15,000? I think so. Is it less than 10,000? Maybe. So far as I am aware, no one has even tried to measure "the news productivity" of quality journalists – not the number of stories generated, but the amount of quality work produced.

Michael: You seem very familiar with new technologies, I'm impressed.

Walter: Well, of course. We do have Wi-Fi where I am.

Michael: In *Liberty and the News*, you wrote that two things might help journalism to nourish democracy. First, you had high hopes that journalism schools would instill in students a professional spirit. And, second, you urged an expansion of outside expertise in data-gathering and political analysis in what you nicely termed "political observatories." How have we done in professionalization inside journalism and the development of political observatories outside?

Walter: Let me take one at a time. First, on professionalization. You are far too young to know just how hopelessly unprofessional journalism was in 1920. There was a strong newsroom prejudice against college education. There was, in fact, a pervasive antipathy to anything that even approached the status of an idea.

And what you and Katherine Fink wrote earlier this year in *Journalism: Theory, Practice and Criticism* about the "rise of contextual journalism" gets the story about right.[2] (Do not be surprised that I keep up with the journals. Digital communication makes this all so easy now.) Almost all of what was printed on the front page well into the 1950s and even into the early 1960s was deferential to power, deficient in energy, and just plain dull. To say that it followed the "5 W's" in an effort at objectivity is a joke. It was 4 W's – who, what, when, where. There was scarcely any effort to examine the "why" of the topic at hand. What Newton Minow would say of television in the 1960s we could well have said of newspapers in 1920 – they were a vast wasteland.

By the late 1960s and the 1970s this had changed dramatically, so that half of the front-page stories became sharply and decisively analytical or interpretive, offering a context for the story that helped frame the particular breaking news event. And after Vietnam, most journalists came to believe that they were not doing their job if they did not offer context.

Michael: But why? Is it that we have more or better journalism schools?

Walter: Journalism schools have improved. I warned in *Liberty and the News* that J-Schools do no good if students are taught by "unenterprising stereotyped minds soaked in the traditions of a journalism always ten years out of date." What matters is "a public recognition of the dignity" of a career in journalism and a training "in which the ideal of objective testimony is cardinal." What is key is that apprentices in journalism become "the patient and fearless men of science who have labored to see what the world really is."[3] This was tougher to achieve by the 1920s than it had been earlier, simply because the world had grown so complicated. And, as I also pointed out, it had grown more complicated within the governmental sphere because the center of government moved from Congress to executive agencies. "It is easier to report Congress than it is to report the departments, because the work of Congress crystallizes crudely every so often in a roll-call. But administration, although it has become more important than legislation, is hard to follow, because its results are spread over a longer period of time and its effects are felt in ways that no reporter can really measure."[4]

Michael: Okay. We'll come back to that. But now back to your solution to the problem of the press. First, you suggested, improve journalism education. And your second key point – outside bureaus of intelligence or political observatories?

Walter: "Theoretically," I wrote, "Congress is competent to act as the critical eye on administration." But that did not happen. Congressional investigations were invariably inadequate to their purposes – they were "almost always planless raids." But two things began happening at the time I wrote. There were "more or less semi-official institutes of government research" established inside government and there was "the growth of specialized private agencies which attempt to give technical summaries of the work of various branches of government." Both are "expert organized reporters."[5] These various organizations collectively – these political observatories – provide analysis that solid news reporters can absorb and retranslate for the public.

In *Public Opinion* I suggested that journalism and journalists are incapable of providing reports adequate to the needs of democracy if they are operating alone, without an adequate "machinery of record" to depend upon. Political observatories are an intermediary with an ongoing and single-minded focus on analyzing and explaining complex political matters in ways accessible to journalists.

Michael: Very well, but it is more than 90 years later now. Have political observatories succeeded?

Walter: All I can say is that political observatories have to succeed. Journalism is not now able to and will never be able to serve democracy without them.

In the long stretch of history from the democracy of ancient Athens to the twenty-first century, popular government has shifted from direct democracy or "assembly" government to "representative" or "republican" government to "monitory" democracy. In what became the United States, "assembly government" was largely limited to local government in New England; the town meeting model never became the template for US state or federal government. At the federal government, representation was the primary governmental form, even though in the beginning the general public voted directly only for the House of Representatives, not the Senate.

But in the twentieth century, something unanticipated happened. The center of gravity in government moved from legislatures to the executive. This was what some thinkers have called "the rise of the administrative state."

But how does the public or its representatives keep an administrative state accountable? The short answer is: "With great difficulty." The longer answer is that a new set of mechanisms has arisen for the purpose – so much so that we might even say, as Australian political theorist John Keane has, that we have a new form of democracy, a "monitory democracy." "Monitory democracy" directs attention to the variety of new ways that power, particularly government power, is monitored by institutions in and out of government, arriving at what Keane calls "the continuous public chastening of those who exercise power."[6] The contrast to representative democracy lies particularly in the term "continuous." Elections offer the occasional public chastening – and monitory democracy could not function without them – but monitory democracy extends the repertoire of mechanisms of oversight that operate day in and day out.

Monitory democracy has emerged, interestingly, both inside and outside the government itself. I saw this beginning to happen in 1919. Outside, think-tanks abound. And, much as I had hoped, universities have sprouted scores of first-rate institutes and schools of public policy that do serious research and analysis. Moreover, independent, for-profit enterprises of public opinion polling add another powerful dimension to all of this.

And government began to monitor itself. The Administrative Procedure Act of 1946, as Judge Richard Posner put it, "signified the acceptance of the administrative state as a legitimate component of the federal lawmaking system, but imposed upon it procedural constraints that have made the administrative process a good deal like the judicial."[7] An amendment to the Administrative Procedure Act passed in 1966 that we know as the Freedom of Information Act. In the post-Watergate era, the Ethics in Government Act of 1978 began the process that led within a few years to the appointment in every Cabinet-level agency and most other major federal agencies of its own office of inspector-general empowered to audit the department on an ongoing basis. The inspectors-general, through semi-annual reports on the agency each monitors, make public an assessment of waste, fraud, and abuse of the public trust. In fiscal 2008, the inspectors-general collectively made recommendations to save over $14 billion, conducted investigations that identified more than $4 billion which the inspectors-general were able to recover, produced more than 6,000 indictments, more than 6,000 successful prosecutions, and nearly 5,000 suspensions and disbarments.[8] By the way, I like how you incorporate the concept of monitory democracy in your new book. And your chapter on the origins of the Freedom of Information Act is illuminating![9]

Michael: Thanks, but how important can these things be? We have had inspectors-general for close to 40 years and nobody knows anything about them!

Walter: True, little in these momentous developments altered civic education. Americans still think they are governed by three co-equal branches of government, period. Even journalists operate on this assumption. For journalists, covering elections, covering the presidency, and covering Congress seemed a full plate as each grew in complexity. The presidential primaries and the "permanent campaign" replaced party conventions for nominations, the president's weight grew as government expanded and as foreign policy became a permanently large feature of presidential responsibility in a leading world power. The operation of Congress, from the 1960s on, became more publicly visible and more internally democratic, less controlled by custom and seniority, more a platform for newer and younger members – and therefore altogether a more difficult story to report.

The bureaucracy, in contrast, was something of a black box, still understood to be concerned with the mechanics of implementing laws originating in the Congress and the White House. Of course, agencies operated with a degree of discretion, but in the conceptual model of democracy Americans unfortunately still work with, administrative discretion is noise in the system more than it is government by design.

The media cover the reports of the offices of the inspector-generals fairly often – but almost never mention what an inspector-general is. What does an inspector-general do? How does an inspector-general come to his or her job? How long is a term of office – if there even is a term of office? What powers does an inspector-general have? Whom does an inspector-general report to? Are the inspector-generals' reports public? I have read at least two dozen *New York Times* news stories over the past several years – I have lots of leisure time to read the paper – with inspector-general reports always properly credited, but in no case has the nature of the inspector-general's office ever been explained, let alone any mention of the relatively recent origin of the office. What an inspector-general does is taken to be just as self-evident as what a senator is or the vice-president or the Speaker of the House or a cabinet secretary. Yet all these other stations in the political firmament have existed since 1789, the inspector-general's office only since a post-Watergate reform of 1978. Journalists do not inform their readers about this, nor, to the best of my knowledge, have media scholars written more than two pages about these and other internal auditors and investigators of government. Yes, I know, those two pages are yours, but shame on you, Michael, they appeared in your article in *Daedalus* and not in a journal that any of your colleagues are likely to read. And, face it, you don't have much of an online presence.

Michael: Well, you can now find that *Daedalus* paper on my Academia.edu page and you can download it from there or from my Columbia Journalism School faculty page.

Walter: Glad to hear it. You really have to keep up, you know.

Michael: You are not the first person to give me this advice – but you are the oldest! One concluding question, and I hate to raise it, but a lot of contemporary critics discuss you as an elitist and an anti-democrat. In Ronald Steel's 1997 preface to *Public Opinion*, he defends you as an ardent democrat: "He not only remained a committed democrat, but he devoted the remainder of his long life to explaining the affairs of state to the general public."

Still, many see you and philosopher John Dewey as adversaries and they side with his warm-hearted Vermont town meeting democrat more than with you.

Walter: Well, I take no responsibility for academics who are sloppy readers. John Dewey read closely, of course. He and I shared a lot – liberalism for one, and faith in science, for another. Both liberalism and science have had hard times in recent decades, not least in the universities. And, let's face it, liberalism and science have a certain cold-heartedness. Liberalism has a stubborn faith in individual rights, due process, and the rule of law, even when they protect scoundrels, and certainly when they protect individuals and minorities from majorities who would use their majority to trample on others. As for science, it does not insist it is always right. Indeed, its ethos is to insist that any conventional wisdom must be revisable and is likely to be revised. Scientific truths do not get written in stone. But science, nonetheless, has strict and unforgiving rules.

So, yes, Professor Dewey was warm-hearted and – for all his brilliance – fuzzy-minded. At least a few critics have read carefully enough to recognize my democratic credentials, you (2008) and Sue Curry Jansen (2012) among them.[10]

Michael: One concluding question. In *Liberty and the News*, you placed great importance on political observatories. That was 1919 and 1920. In *Public Opinion*, published in 1922, the phrase "political observatories" does not appear. You note, as before, the failures of the press to make the invisible world visible except in those cases where other institutions by their nature provide a useful machinery of record – sports scores and stock market quotations. What happened to political observatories?

Walter: Well, I do not like to repeat myself. And I was increasingly concerned about the growing role of the public relations man in those years. These people peddled soft-core propaganda to promote special interests. They might have training in journalism, they might have a veneer of knowledgeability, but they were counterfeits in the circulation of information for democracy.

But my anxiety about the influence of public relations on journalism was not the whole of my analysis. Just about everybody has ignored the penultimate paragraph of what I wrote on the press in *Public Opinion*. The second sentence of that paragraph has been much cited – "It [the press] is like the beam of a searchlight that moves restlessly about, bringing one episode and then another out of darkness into vision." But this sentence makes sense only in relationship to the sentence that precedes it: "The press is no substitute for institutions." And that is why, a few sentences further on, I wrote, "The trouble lies deeper than the press, and so does the remedy. It lies in social organization based on a system of analysis and record…Then…the news is uncovered for the press by a system of intelligence that is also a check upon the press." Well, pardon me for quoting myself. But, without being too smug about it, I don't see a word in those sentences I would change.[11]

Michael: So do we have today a "system of intelligence that is also a check upon the press"?

Walter: Time will tell. But I think there is reason for optimism. The internet has enabled a kind of crowd-sourced check upon the press, pointing out its omissions and its errors. New fact-checking organizations focus particularly on misstatements by politicians and political candidates, but they also "fact-check" leading media outlets. People worry about how easy it is today for citizens to live in separate and polarized ideological and partisan informational neighborhoods. But I am rather impressed by the sheer weight of information circulating. And, remember, it is just so much easier for people to "fact-check" themselves! You think you read such-and-such in the paper a few days ago, but someone has doubted your rendition of it. Well, even if you read it in print and the print got thrown in the recycling bin that has gone off to the recycling center, you just go online and find it. Information hangs around much longer than it used to. Even some old ghosts hang around longer than one might have expected.

Michael: I'm glad that's true! Thanks for granting this interview today.

Walter: Happy to do it.

3

Is Journalism a Profession?
Objectivity 1.0, Objectivity 2.0,
and Beyond

This chapter draws on ideas about the professionalization of American journalism that I have explored in work going back to my first book, *Discovering the News: A Social History of American Newspapers*, in 1978. Here I have reformulated them in a way I think helps clarify how professionalism in journalism has shifted over time, and how it is that journalists can be both devoted to factuality at the same time that they are increasingly committed to fair-minded interpretation or "contextualizing" in presenting news. At a time when the mainstream or self-consciously professional news media, whether in print, on radio, on television, or in various digital formats, is under broad, demagogic attack in the United States and elsewhere, what seemed to me a matter of historical interest has again become a topic of political urgency.

Lee Bollinger became president of Columbia University in mid-2002, not long after Tom Goldstein announced he was stepping down as dean at Columbia Journalism School. A search committee had arrived at a short-list of distinguished candidates for a successor to Goldstein, but President Bollinger announced that he was suspending the search to give the school time to think through "the role of a journalism school at a first-rate university." What the J-School at Columbia did very well, by most accounts – training in skills – was certainly important, Bollinger acknowledged, but a deeper education in the substantive issues journalists must cover, taking advantage of a deeper integration with the rest of the university, was on his mind. Bollinger took journalism very seriously – not only as a noted First Amendment scholar but as someone who grew up in a newspaper family, his father the proprietor of a small-town paper. Bollinger convened a taskforce to consider the direction that a "pre-eminent school of journalism" should take in the contemporary world.

In April, 2003, Bollinger declared that a graduate education in journalism should take longer than 10 months and should go beyond training in basic skills. He announced the appointment of a new dean, Nicholas Lemann, who had been involved in the taskforce meetings, and who believed in the value of lengthening a graduate journalism education to two years. Journalists needed to know more, and more deeply, the subject areas they covered. They should take courses at the university outside the Journalism School, a practically seditious idea in journalism education at that time. Neither President Bollinger nor Dean Lemann focused on specific technological changes in and around journalism.

The idea of making journalism education more academic was not warmly greeted among journalists. *Washington Post* and *Newsweek* columnist Robert Samuelson immediately responded that Bollinger's vision amounted to a drive to build "snob journalism" – "journalism by an elite for an elite." For Samuelson, "journalism is best learned by doing it." Journalism schools? At best "necessary evils." He found Bollinger's vision pretentious, its attitude toward working journalists condescending. And his choice of Lemann did not make things any better. Though Samuelson acknowledged Lemann to be "a brilliant writer, an exhaustive reporter, a gifted thinker," his specialty was "long reflective articles for upscale (aka elite) publications with comparatively small circulations" – all very well, Samuelson suggested, but not what most reporters do.[1] Samuelson's concerns did not focus on new technology any more than Bollinger's or Lemann's; he worried that the audience for news was shrinking and young people especially were moving to entertainment fare, not news, although he briefly notes that part of the decline among the young was a move to internet news sites.

Dean Lemann recruited me to teach at Columbia Journalism School in 2005. I am not a player in the story of curriculum reform at Columbia, but I just want to locate myself in relation to these events. I had not paid much attention to technological change either. I had reluctantly given up my IBM Selectric typewriter for a desktop computer somewhere in the 1980s, and had worked on a desktop computer for some 20 years by the time I came to Columbia. I was also an enthusiastic convert to email. I bought my first laptop in 2006 when I started at Columbia, and my first cellphone at about the same time, in both cases to help manage the communicative complications of holding academic appointments simultaneously in California and New York, since I maintained my position at the University of California, San Diego for several years thereafter. At that time, Facebook had been founded, but it would not be a general commercial service until the following year. YouTube had just launched. There was no Twitter. There was no iPhone until 2007. Wikipedia was four years old and would a year later reach one million articles in its English edition, more than three million five years later. Like many other academics, I spoke with disdain about Wikipedia – while gradually making more and more use of it myself and before long coming to recognize it as a modern marvel.

In journalism, 2005 seems a very long time ago. That is a problem. It is a problem for understanding where journalism has come from, even for grasping what journalism is, not to mention imagining where it might be going. Today, the power of digital media is so blinding that everything that came before it seems to be blended into one food-processed mush. From Ben Franklin at the *Pennsylvania Gazette* through 240 years to Ben Bradlee at the *Washington Post* overseeing Bob Woodward and Carl Bernstein on Watergate, all of that was suddenly the undifferentiated "old days," replaced in a flash by the only change in journalism we seem able to recall – from the old days to a journalism more fragmented, more horizontal, more snarky, more opinionated, more tabloid, more rapid-fire, more transparent, more interactive, more participatory, more multimedia, more just about everything except financially rewarding. In the blink of an eye, what people (mistakenly) took to be a longstanding, professionalized journalistic world where journalists stood as leading authorities on newsworthiness and offered a sophisticated, detached grasp of the mechanics and machinations of political life simply caved in.

Much in journalism is changing today, and changing quickly, but it is not changing from a venerable profession with a long-settled set of practices.

"Profession" is a term with a familiar popular meaning. Its meaning in sociology is, in the end, not very different from popular usage. In both cases there is something appealing and at the same time off-putting about the notion of profession. It is appealing because it is honorific. A "professional" has a halo. If you are a professional, you are knowledgeable and skillful at what you do. You are no amateur – you do what you do well and people pay you to do it. You are a "real pro." To call oneself a professional is to claim status, and to expect from others high regard, trust, and deference to one's expertise and trained judgment, be they manifested in well-honed skills or mastery of a complex body of knowledge.

Professionals do not always make good on their claims to expert judgment, as both sociologists and the general public know. So we know versions of George Bernard Shaw's line: "Every profession is a conspiracy against the laity." We know this about doctors, we know it about lawyers. And we surely know it about journalists, although we may never have accepted that journalism is a professional activity in the first place – indeed, journalists themselves have been ambivalent about embracing a professional identity. But today more than ever, it is important to understand something about the process of professionalization that journalism has gone through in the past 100 years, including notable changes that have taken place since the 1960s, and to think clearly about where journalism might go, or should go, from where it is today.

In journalism, as in other fields, the question of professional standing becomes sensitive at moments when the boundaries of the field are difficult to police and the deference attached to the professional occupation, either in law or in public recognition, is wavering. At these moments – and clearly this is such a moment now in journalism – the meaning of professionalism becomes a subject of considerable interest. If we look back to the beginnings of newspapers in the 1600s and 1700s, journalism was not a profession anywhere in the world. It was not a distinct occupation – nor even a full-time occupation. It was only in the 1800s, and primarily in the second half of that century, that journalism became a full-time job – in fact, a set of differentiated full-time jobs – and it was only then that journalism became aware of itself as an occupational field with distinctive social habits, gathering spots, organizations, a few journals for and about itself, books of instruction for self-help, adult education, and even some college classes. This is not to say that journalism as a self-conscious field was evenly distributed across the various organizations that published news. Until 1920, a majority of American lived in rural areas, small towns, and pint-sized cities, not in major urban centers like New York and Atlanta and Detroit. There were newspapers, usually weeklies, in thousands of small towns, but they were of small size and modest ambition, dependent on reader contributions to fill the pages, and normally reluctant to cover controversial topics. They were community newsletters more than independent newspapers. It was only in the cities, and particularly in New York and Chicago, that journalism was a large enough field to recognize itself and organize itself.

Where the history of other professions is typically about the development of higher education organized on behalf of the profession and the emergence of self-governing associations of professionals with the power to limit entry to their field, gain recognition from the state, and formally or informally discipline their own members, the story of how journalism became a profession is about journalism finding its own voice. This happened without journalism having ever attained the kind of self-organizing power to be found in law or medicine and without having attained or even aspired to the glow of professional status. Robert Samuelson hated Bollinger's explicit hope that journalism should be a "profession." That is simply a "bad idea," he wrote; it would "reduce journalism's relevance and raise public mistrust." But journalism had already been professionalized, twice-over. It came to have something like professionalism, including a plausible claim to expertise, from the late nineteenth century on, and it took a second professionalizing leap after 1965. The location of both these professionalizing developments was the metropolitan daily newspaper newsroom, formal schooling taking at most a secondary role. Both of these steps toward professionalism – that I am about to describe in more detail – brought forth distinctive tools for reporting and writing news, loosely linked to an ethic for resisting the siren songs of the marketplace (despite its residence inside the newspaper in the business office) and the government.[2]

The Emergence of Journalism as an Occupational Field

Until the late 1800s, at the earliest, journalism was not a profession. Only late in the nineteenth century and early in the twentieth century did newspapers make a substantial investment in information-gathering, especially in foreign correspondents. The British and American news worlds could both boast of leading newspapers with teams of foreign correspondents as early as the 1850s, although France had no newspaper with foreign correspondents before the 1870s and most French newspapers had none until 1914. Media scholar Jean Chalaby declares on this basis that modern journalism is an "Anglo-American invention." And Chalaby argues further that the Anglo-American press developed "fact-centred discursive practices" and so gave journalism "its specificity as a class of texts."[3] It was not just an investment in information, but the invention of ways of gathering it and presenting it in a mode that was not politics, not philosophy, not polemic, and not literature. It was a news-centered, news-obsessed set of practices and textual forms called journalism.

Part of this was the evolution of distinctive work practices. The most notable was interviewing. "The interview," British journalist William Stead acknowledged in 1902, "was a distinctively American invention."[4] Something of the novelty of the practice can be recognized in Mark Twain's characteristically sardonic report in 1868:

> I came across one of the lions of the country today at the Senate – General Sherman. The conversation I had with this gentleman therefore ought to be reported, I suppose. I said the weather was very fine, and he said he had seen finer. Not liking to commit myself further, in the present unsettled conditions of politics, I said good morning. Understanding my little

game, he said good morning also. This was all that passed, but it was very significant. It reveals clearly what he thinks of impeachment. I regard this manner of getting a great man's opinions a little underhanded, but then everybody does it.[5]

Not everybody did interviews in 1868. But in the United States, they would all be doing so by the 1890s. Thompson Cooper, correspondent for the *New York World*, in 1871 became the first journalist in the world to interview the Pope (Pius IX). The newspaper wrote the following as preface to the story:

> The Roman Catholic Church is the oldest, as the interview is almost the youngest, of the institutions of mankind. And they are this morning presented face to face in the persons of their respective representatives – his Holiness Pius IX and Mr. Thompson Cooper upon the part of *The World* of New York. The spirit of the Church and the spirit of the age, in concrete and accurate types, have met together. The Church and the Press have kissed each other.[6]

This pretentiously identifies the interview as one of the "institutions" of mankind, but that gets it about right. The interview was a new institution, both as a social interaction between reporters and politicians or celebrities and as a nonfiction literary text, a new organization of prose.

At about the same time, journalistic narrative moved from chronological accounts of recent happenings to news-centered news stories – stories that is, that began with a summary lead (or "lede") to emphasize what the reporter and a consensus of journalists understood among themselves to be the most important features of the reported events. This shift is very clear in the changing modes of news accounts of the president's annual "State of the Union" address. Only gradually did the news story move from being exclusively the full verbatim statement by the president, along with a chronological account of proceedings in the Congress the day of the delivery of the message, to a report that placed first the reporter's account of what was the most important part of the president's message.[7]

Before the 1880s or so in the US and 1920 or so in the UK, journalists were one voice among many in the newspapers; and they were often subordinated to political factions or politi-

cal parties or government officials. They were not *the* interpreting agent in the papers, but one among many, and they
were not representing a distinctively journalistic point of view.
Newspapers were little more than aggregators of a variety of
acceptable public voices. Newspapers were a miscellany of
tones, styles, and voices.

On this point, British scholar Donald Matheson is especially
instructive. He begins a brilliant essay on the modernization
of British journalism by citing the lead sentence of a story in
The Times of London in 1901 that epitomizes a nineteenth-
century journalism that would soon be antique and that no
reporter could conceivably write today: "We have this morning
to make the startling announcement that the Chancellor of
the Exchequer has placed his resignation in the hands of Lord
Salisbury."[8] The sentence makes sense only if a certain cultural
climate is taken for granted, one in which offices matter more
than their incumbents and so the personal name of the Chancellor of the Exchequer does not have to be provided. (Alternatively, perhaps the target audience for *The Times* was small
enough and homogeneous enough that the writer could safely
assume that anyone discerning enough to read *The Times* in
the first place did not have to be reminded of the name of the
incumbent Chancellor of the Exchequer). It is a culture in
which the obligation of the newspaper to provide startling
announcements is not fully understood as the mission of the
paper and so it has to be self-consciously declared. The "we"
calls attention to the newspaper as a corporate enterprise that
is acting in the world rather than taking for granted that it
is a machinery that stands to the side and describes or inter-
prets the world.

It is not that journalists were competing so much with
alternative information sources available in other venues – in
almanacs or sermons or songs or handbills. It is that newspapers themselves were such a miscellany of sources, styles,
and authors that, as Matheson argues, the newspaper rarely
narrated the world "in its own voice. In fact, it did not really
have a voice."[9] Nor were reporters even in a position to frame
the words of others. Editors did not edit reports from correspondents – the latter were printed complete as submitted,
as were reports of the proceedings of courts or of Parliament,
speeches at public meetings, and so forth. All of this suggests

that "journalism did not yet have the tools or the authority to redefine the context of words." Only when it acquired these tools did journalism become "a form of knowledge in itself, not dependent on other discourses to be able to make statements about the world."[10]

Journalism, by World War I, did not require any formal education anywhere in the world. In the United States, until about that time, a college education was said to be a handicap for a young man (or the very few young women) aspiring to a job on a newspaper. Certainly, these young people did not need mastery of any particular body of knowledge, let alone an "abstract" body of knowledge or "abstract" principles, often said to be the mark of an occupation of professional standing. Those who earned a living as journalists – which is to say, who wrote for or reported or took photographs for newspapers or news-oriented magazines – did not control conditions of their own employment; they did not have a formal ethical code, they did not normally belong to any organizations in their capacity as reporters, and they did not share a high status relative to other occupational groups. But reporters were becoming full-time, paid workers. They were developing a sense of an occupational identity they were proud to call their own. And they were developing social practices they learned on the job that distinguished them from others who wrote for publication outside journalism.[11]

Still, the old ways hung on, in some places for a very long time. In the Netherlands, Dutch media historian Marcel Broersma argues, newspapers were arranged in a "vertical" format until after 1945. The pages were nothing but gray – no illustrations, no photographs, nothing one could really call a headline. The first story began at the top of the left-hand column. If it finished mid-column, a short line would separate it from the next story that followed in the same column. Perhaps that story ran about two columns. It would go from the lower half of column one to the top of column two, down to the bottom of that column and up to the top of column three and finish somewhere in the middle of that column. The next story, after a short line, would then begin in the lower portion of column three. And so forth.

What's missing from this? The answer should be apparent: editors and readers. No one was exercising any sort of editorial judgment and no one was making any effort to market the news to readers. The front-page familiar to American readers in the last decades of the nineteenth century and British readers by about 1920 was unknown to Dutch newspaper consumers for decades thereafter. The Anglo-American front-page distinguishes more important from less important stories by page placement, headline font size, number of columns the headline spans, sidebars, and so forth. But until 1945 Dutch journalists did not presume to tell readers what the most important information was; they typically offered a chronicle of events without extracting the news from it. In the Netherlands, it was not until after 1945 that there was anything that *looked* like what we have come to accept as modern journalism.[12]

The Rise of Journalism's "High Modernity": Objectivity 1.0

Journalism's finding of its voice has not just been a matter of vanquishing other voices in the newspaper or claiming the authority to frame others' voices on radio, television, or in print. It has also been about attaining the legitimacy to speak in public on matters of political importance. This varies across national political cultures. Consider the British "14-day" rule. It survived only from World War II until 1957, but it is instructive. In the 14-day rule, the BBC, by agreement with both political parties, would not broadcast news or commentary on any issue that Parliament planned to debate within the coming 14 days. In 1955 the Postmaster-General, who oversaw the BBC, replaced this informal constraint on news with a formal prohibition. At this, the BBC rebelled and said that decisions on how to present current affairs was their responsibility, not that of the parties or anyone else. Prime Minister Winston Churchill disagreed: "It would be shocking to have debates in the House forestalled, time after time, by expressions of opinion by persons who had not the status or responsibility of MPs." Others in Parliament agreed that the parties, not the BBC, should decide these matters. Both parties objected that MPs would be "pressurized" by broadcasts within the 14 days and feared the BBC might select "non-representative speakers" who might "discuss issues where Parliament alone had the right to decide."[13]

The question of whether journalism becomes a relatively professional field is in part the question of whether journalistic discourse becomes distinct from other forms of publication and other forms of talk. For this to happen, journalists must begin to talk to one another, not just to wider audiences. They must enter into a world structured by distinct occupational norms, values, and practices. Full professionalization requires this, but also much more. Physicians often have, but journalists do not, significant control over the conditions of their own employment and a high degree of control over access to membership in the field. There is little disagreement that physicians are collectively dedicated to a public function (serving to improve the health of individuals in society); there is some agreement, but not so uniform, that journalism does – or at least should – serve a public function of providing individuals the information they need to participate intelligently in democracy. While journalists often pat themselves on the back for serving in a field that is essential to democracy and that puts the public good above parochial interests, even a casual observer sympathetic to excellent journalism can see that this explains very little of very many news publications around the world, even if it explains a significant portion of a very small number of distinguished news organizations.

So the process of professionalization in journalism has been incomplete at best. Still, it did reach a first definitional moment – call it Objectivity 1.0 – when it accepted a definition of what it meant to be independent from the state and the market. A significant date would be 1923, when the American Society of Newspaper Editors, just founded in 1922, wrote up its code of ethics and urged dedication to nonpartisan reporting of the facts of the matter at hand. The term "objectivity" came into the common vocabulary of American journalism for the first time in the 1920s and received glowing praise and some valuable exegetical philosophizing from journalist and public intellectual Walter Lippmann. At the same time, the faith in objectivity rested – explicitly in Lippmann's writing – on the recognition that journalists were surrounded by and preyed upon by all kinds of propagandists and public relations agents who sought to persuade them or bribe them or flatter them to favor one or another cause in their stories. Objectivity as a practice was, as sociologist Gaye Tuchman would later characterize it, a "defensive strategic ritual."[14]

That's quite right – but incomplete. Objectivity also became a belief. As media historian John Nerone has observed, "Journalism is an ism. That is, it is a belief system. In particular, it is the belief system that defines the appropriate practices and values of news professionals, news media, and news systems."[15] If that is too strong, media scholar Barbie Zelizer has labeled the set of ideas, attitudes, and practices that most American and many other journalists share, an "interpretive community."[16]

The first era of professionalization, then, crystallized in the 1920s and reached a peak in the 1950s and 1960s, the era of journalism's "high modernity," as media scholar Daniel Hallin named it.[17] Here, "objectivity" was widely identified as an ideal and the routines of journalism as practices dedicated to it. But while rhetorical combat continues to this day over the pros and cons of Objectivity 1.0 (now often called condescendingly "he said/she said" journalism), news organizations and news-writing have moved on to something importantly new, beginning in the 1960s and culminating quickly in the 1970s, that we may think of as Objectivity 2.0.

The Coming of Objectivity 2.0

As virtually all accounts by journalists and historians attest, American news coverage of government, politics, and society opened up in the 1960s and 1970s. It was not the U-2 incident, or the Kennedy–Nixon debates; it was not any specific skirmish, or even the sum of the confrontations between the press and US military spokesmen in Vietnam as the war there dragged on; it was not the rise in the 1960s of irreverent underground publications, or the growing respect for maverick reporter I. F. Stone, who became a hero for politically committed young reporters of the day. It was all of this and more. There was no single turning point – certainly not Watergate. Seymour Hersh's breaking of the story of the My Lai massacre and other notable investigative reporting on the Vietnam war preceded Watergate. Take nothing away from Woodward and

Bernstein and the *Washington Post*'s pursuit of the Watergate story, but the change in journalism cannot be hung on a single event, no matter how shattering. Something deeper was at stake. There was a generational change, a broad cultural change, and a refashioning of how to understand democracy that all contributed to making the news media a chief agent in the opening up of American society.

The change in the media's role was the joint product of several closely connected developments: government – especially the federal government – grew larger and more engaged in people's everyday lives; the culture of journalism changed and journalists asserted themselves more aggressively than before; and many governmental institutions became less secretive and more attuned to the news media, eager for media attention and approval. As the federal government expanded its reach (in civil rights, economic regulation, environmental responsibility, and social welfare programs like food stamps, Medicare, and Medicaid), as the women's movement proclaimed that "the personal is political," and as stylistic innovations in journalism proved a force of their own, the very concept of "covering politics" changed, too.

News coverage became at once more probing, more analytical, and more transgressive of conventional lines between public and private, but even this recognizes only part of what influenced a changing journalism. Not only did the news media grow in independence and professionalism and provide a more comprehensive and more critical coverage of powerful institutions, but powerful institutions adapted to a world in which journalists had a more formidable presence than ever before. Of course, politicians had resented the press much earlier – President George Washington complained about how he was portrayed in the newspapers; President Thomas Jefferson encouraged libel prosecutions in the state courts against editors who attacked him and his policies; and President Theodore Roosevelt, a pioneer among presidents in manipulating journalists, famously castigated the negative tone of reporters he dubbed "muckrakers."[18] Even so, Washington politics remained much more exclusively an insiders' game than it would be later. The Washington press corps was more subservient to the whims and wishes of editors and publishers back home than to official Washington and, in any event, politicians in

Washington kept their jobs less by showing themselves in the best light in the newspapers than by maintaining their standing among their party's movers and shakers in their home state. Members of the US Senate were not popularly elected until 1914; before then, a remoteness from popular opinion was a senator's birthright. And while in the early twentieth century a small number of writers at the most influential newspapers and a small number of syndicated political columnists came to be influential power brokers, the press as a corporate force did not have an imposing presence.

Presence is what the media acquired by the late 1960s. It was in part manufactured by the Nixon administration's insistence on referring to what had generally been known as "the press" as "the media," a term that Nixon insiders judged to be conveniently more distancing and forbidding than "the press."[19] Presence did not mean a seat at the table, but an internalization in the minds of political decision-makers that the media were alert, powerful, and by no means sympathetic. Partially independent of how journalists covered Washington (and other centers of political power), those who held political power came to orient themselves in office, or in seeking office, to public opinion and to their belief that the media both reflected and influenced it.[20]

Media coverage of Congress in the 1950s and into the 1960s had been, as one contemporary gently called it, "over-cooperative."[21] One reporter on Capitol Hill said (in 1956) that covering the Senate was "a little like being a war correspondent; you really become a part of the outfit you are covering."[22]

Such politician–journalist collaboration was standard practice.[23] "Until the mid-1960s," as Julian Zelizer, a leading historian of Congress, simply observes, "the press was generally respectful of the political establishment."[24] The decline of this respect helped bring more attention to political scandal. Scandal reporting, frequently decried as a lowering of the standards of the press from serious coverage of issues to a frivolous and sensational focus on political sideshows, is nonetheless a symptom of a system that had become more democratic. As governing became more public (through the Freedom of Information Act in 1966, the Legislative Reorganization Act of

1970 bringing more "sunshine" to Congress, the National Environmental Policy Act of 1970 requiring federal agencies to provide and publicly release "environmental impact statements," the campaign finance laws of 1971 and 1974, the Inspectors General Act of 1978, and other legislative milestones), politicians and government officers were more often held accountable.[25] The character of democracy shifted from one in which voters normally could express and act on disapproval of government incumbents only on election day to one in which, in Zelizer's words, "the nation would no longer have to wait until an election to punish government officials, nor would it have to depend on politicians to decide when an investigation was needed."[26] To some extent, the proliferation of scandals was made possible by the new information that political candidates were required by law to report or that legislation newly insisted that the executive branch of government make publicly available. More broadly, scandal reporting increased with the growing acceptance of values promoted by the women's movement that blurred the line between public and private behavior or, to put it more strongly, demonstrated that that line had been an artificial construction, and a gendered one, all along.

Analysis of newspaper content over time shows that there has been an increase in investigative reporting in and after the late 1960s, as popular history and personal recollections anticipate, but that increase is quantitatively modest when measured as a percentage of all front-page news stories. More surprising, because less a part of how journalists picture their own past, there has been a stunning growth in what I think is best called "contextual reporting." As Kathy Roberts Forde has observed, there is no standard terminology for this kind of journalism. It has been called interpretative reporting, depth reporting, long-form journalism, explanatory reporting, and analytical reporting.[27] In his extensive interviewing of Washington journalists in the late 1970s, Stephen Hess called it "social science journalism," a mode of reporting with "the accent on greater interpretation" and a clear intention of focusing on causes, not on events as such.[28] Although this kind of reporting – the centerpiece of Objectivity 2.0 – is, in quantitative terms, easily the most important change in reporting in the past three-quarters of a century up to the rise of online journalism, it has neither a settled name nor a hallowed place in journalism's understanding of its own past.

Four propositions summarize much of the available evidence that over the past half century there has been a shift in the content of journalism and in the culture of the newsrooms that produce it: (1) news stories grew longer; (2) they grew more critical of established power; (3) journalists came to present themselves publicly as more aggressive; and (4) news offered more context for understanding the events of the day. The highlights of these propositions follow.

First, *news stories have grown longer*. One well-documented study, by Kevin Barnhurst and Diana Mutz, shows that newspaper stories have become longer over time. Sampling the *New York Times*, the *Chicago Tribune*, and *The (Portland) Oregonian* every twentieth year from 1894 through 1994, Barnhurst and Mutz find a consistently increasing mean length of news stories in all three papers, in all three categories of stories that they examined (accidents, crimes, and job-related stories) across the whole time-span of their study – 1894 to 1994. The three papers showed little change from 1914 to 1934; the *Oregonian* shows a notable increase in length by 1954 and all three papers – *The Times* especially – show growing story length between 1954 and 1974. Stories in *The Times* and the *Oregonian* continued to lengthen in 1994, although the increases are modest; *The Tribune* story length decreased between 1974 and 1994, but remained higher than in any of the years measured from 1894 through 1954.[29]

Barnhurst and Mutz do not certify that the longer stories of 1974 and 1994 offer "better" journalism than the shorter stories of 1954 and earlier, but it is hard not to believe that, in general, they do.

Second, *news has grown more critical of established power*. Looking at ten mainstream metropolitan dailies from 1963 to 1964 and 1998 to 1999 (sampling two weeks in each period) from different regions of the country, media analyst and *American Journalism Review* columnist Carl Sessions Stepp wrote: "To read 1963 newspapers is to re-enter a pre-Watergate, pre-Vietnam, pre-Dealey Plaza world. It is to roll back a gigantic cultural loss of idealism." According to Stepp, newspapers in this earlier period seemed "naively trusting of government, shamelessly boosterish, unembarrassedly hokey and obliging." He was surprised to find stories "often not attributed at all, simply passing along an unquestioned, quasi-official sense of things. The worldview seemed white, male, middle-aged and middle class, a comfortable and confident Optimist Club bonhomie."[30] This was very different from what he found in his 1998–9 sample. Today, journalists sometimes celebrate critical judgment and a watchdog's instinct for the soft underbelly of politicians as if they were part of a long tradition, but Stepp's analysis finds little evidence of any of these features in the content of 1963–4 newspapers.

Stepp concludes that the 1999 papers were "by almost any measure, far superior to their 1960s counterparts." They were "better written, better looking, better organized, more responsible, less sensational, less sexist and racist, and more informative and public-spirited."[31] Less idiosyncratic, with less aroma of a particular locale, these papers provided more nutritional fare by any measure.

Third, *journalists have come to present themselves publicly as aggressive*. In a rich series of research papers, sociolinguists Steven Clayman and John Heritage and their colleagues analyzed the questions reporters have asked in presidential press conferences from 1953 through 2000. They find significant increases in "initiative" (prefacing a question with statements to construct a particular context, asking multiple questions within a single turn, or asking a follow-up question), in "assertiveness" (inviting a particular answer – "isn't it true that...? or "don't you think that...?"); and in "adversarialness" ("Mr. President, Senator So-and-So has criticized your Policy X as disastrous for the economy, national defense, and American morals – how do you respond?") There was a notable rise on all of these measures of aggressiveness in 1969 and at no point after 1969 did the heightened level of aggressive questioning return to the more deferential questioning style that prevailed during the Eisenhower, Kennedy, and Johnson administrations.

Fourth, *news has grown more contextual*. Max Frankel, Washington bureau chief for the *New York Times* from 1968 to 1972 and the *Times* executive editor from 1988 to 1994, recalls a growing pressure in the 1960s to offer "something unique" that other news outlets did not provide. This meant more analysis or more of a "mood" piece like "'what France is up to' or 'what Hitler represents' and so on." This was acceptable even decades earlier for foreign correspondents, but rarely for national or local news reporters. Abe Rosenthal, managing editor of *The Times* in the 1970s and executive editor for most of the 1980s, liked to encourage good writing and practiced it himself in his days as a foreign correspondent. "He was a brilliant stylist," Frankel has recalled, and master of "the so-called soft but significant lead." As editor, Rosenthal was "very tolerant of well-written, correspondent-like stories even when they came from the Bronx. Not just from India." Frankel recalls that in his own tenure as editor he was "insistent" in his effort "to get analysis into regular news stories."[32]

News stories have grown more contextualized over time, less confined to describing the immediately observable here-and-now. In 1960 more than 90 percent of *New York Times* front-page stories concerning electoral campaigns were largely descriptive – but this figure was less than 20 percent by 1992, according to Thomas Patterson's research.[33] Reporters took a more active part in their own stories, and not to the benefit of candidates for office.

In his further analysis of the *New York Times*, *Chicago Tribune*, and the *Oregonian*, Barnhurst found a small decrease from 1894 (25 percent) to 1914 (22 percent) to 1934 (21 percent) in the proportion of front-page stories that refer to the past rather than only to the temporally immediate context (hours or days) of the event the stories focus on. Thereafter there are large increases in references to the past in the stories – 28 percent in 1954, 39 percent in 1954, and 49 percent in 1994.[34]

Katherine Fink and I have added to this portrait of an emerging Objectivity 2.0 an analysis of the content of three newspapers: the *New York Times*, the *Washington Post*, and the *Milwaukee Journal Sentinel*.[35] We examined articles on the front pages of each newspaper over two weeks in the years 1955, 1967, 1979, 1991, and 2003, distinguishing conventional stories (event-centered information that addresses the who, what, when, and where of the event) from contextual stories (that emphasize "why" and provide information that the reporter judges to be part of the appropriate context for understanding the significance of the event at hand).

In our analysis, conventional stories often, though not always, focus on the official activities of government. This category includes stories about lawmaking and politics, but also public safety, such as court prosecutions, police crime reports, responses to fires, and natural disasters. A conventional story, however, is defined not by its subject matter but by its approach. Three features stand out. First, a conventional story identifies its subject clearly and promptly. Commonly, these stories answer the "who-what-when-where" questions in the lead paragraph or even the lead sentence. Also, commonly, the stories ignore or only implicitly address the "why" question. They tend to be written in the "inverted pyramid" style, with the most important information coming first.

Second, the conventional story describes activities that have occurred or will occur within 24 hours. (In some cases, the activities may have occurred earlier but were not publicly known until very recently.) One giveaway of a conventional story is a lead paragraph with the word "yesterday" or "today." Contextual stories may focus on an occurrence of the past 24 hours but just as often may center on an event, action, or trend that runs over a longer time period or offers background for some trigger activity of the past day or two or three.

Third, conventional stories focus on one-time activities or actions – discrete events rather than long-term processes or sequences. This includes planned events, such as public meetings, as well as unplanned events like accidents or natural disasters. These activities may not be events in the world, but rather statements about them made by a powerful person, either in public or in speaking with a reporter. Contextual stories, in contrast, tend to focus on the big picture, providing context or background for a topic of current interest. Where the conventional story is a well-cropped, tightly focused shot, the contextual story uses a wide-angle lens. It is often explanatory in nature, sometimes appearing beside conventional stories to complement the dry, just-the-facts versions of that day's events. Sometimes, newspapers label contextual stories "news analysis," as if to head off anticipated criticism that these stories mix interpretation with facts. Contextual stories are often written in the present tense, since they describe processes and activities that are ongoing rather than events that have been both initiated and completed in the preceding hours or days. Alternatively, they may be written in the past tense, if their purpose is to give historical context.

Obviously, contextual stories are not all alike. They may be explanatory stories that help readers better understand complicated issues. They may be trend stories, using numerical data to show change over time on matters of public interest like high school graduation rates, population growth, or unemployment. There are also descriptive stories that engage the imaginations of readers, transporting them to unfamiliar places. These are not travel pieces – they describe places that are newsworthy, not likely family vacation sites.

Descriptive contextual articles are not always about places far from home. A *New York Times* article from 1991 describes two competing images of Newark, New Jersey: "one of gleaming steel and glass towers, the other of 100-year-old railroad shacks and multifamily wood frame houses in neighborhoods with few stores or amenities, not even a movie theater." There are different ways to offer context; what all contextual stories share is an effort at offering accounts that go behind or beyond the "who-what-when-where" of a recent or unfolding event.

Consider a front-page story on the US economic recovery in the *New York Times*, May 5, 2012. The "news peg" – a specific in-the-past-24-hours point of reference – was the monthly press release from the US Bureau of Labor Statistics on employment trends. According to the Bureau, employment in April rose by 115,000 jobs and the unemployment rate was unchanged. The press release did not say that job creation in April was less than half of what it had been in the first months of the year. It did not say that the proportion of working-age Americans either working or looking for work was lower than at any time since 1981. It did not say the proportion of men in the labor force fell to 70 percent in April, the lowest figure since the government began collecting this information in 1948. It was not the government press release, but reporter Catherine Rampell who provided readers with all this comparative information. She turned a tepid government press release into a front-page story, underscoring that the economic situation remained dismal.

Was this too interpretive? Did it offer too much of Rampell's own opinion, all but declaring that the Obama administration's optimistic press release was misleading? How sure was she that she had consulted the right assortment of economists? Was she too critical of the beleaguered Obama administration trying desperately to revive the sinking economy it had inherited from George W. Bush? Different people may assess this differently, but there seems little doubt that Rampell was conscientiously pursuing what from the 1970s on had become the generally accepted obligation of Objectivity 2.0 journalists – to not take government statements at face value, to recognize them as tendentious (even if in a narrow sense true), and to work to provide a context that fair-minded and informed observers would regard as appropriate.

Table 3.1 summarizes what Katherine Fink and I found overall across the samples we examined from the *New York Times*, the *Washington Post*, and the *Milwaukee Journal* over five time periods. From 1979 on, it is clear that contextual journalism has played a major role in the newspapers, representing a third (and by 1991 half) of the front-page stories across the three papers. None of the papers – the *Milwaukee Journal* comparable to its more famous nationally oriented counterparts – is any longer committed only to the pared-down, just-the-facts "he said, she said" of the 1950s. A much larger part is what Fink and I have called "contextual journalism." It offers interpretation and analysis in its stories – not partisan analysis, but contextual information and framing to help readers set the events of the day in a context that makes them comprehensible.

What brought about Objectivity 2.0? In the United States, Objectivity 2.0 was provoked by the Vietnam war and capped by Watergate, but it was also encouraged by a huge expansion of higher education and the centrality there of a "critical" or even "adversary" culture, and a broad rebellion – around the

Table 3.1

	Conventional	Contextual	Investigative	Other
1955	85%	9%	0%	7%
1967	79%	17%	0%	4%
1979	60%	33%	1%	6%
1991	51%	47%	3%	0%
2003	47%	51%	1%	0%

world – against "the Establishment." Journalism became less comfortable with its role as part of the Establishment. The habit of identifying with political insiders began to be embarrassing. The roles of "watchdog," independent critic, and accountability warden became more congenial. The smug self-assurance of 1950s journalism has never entirely disappeared, but professionalism as a set of values now incorporates assumptions about a dividing line between politicians and journalists that was much less true in the 1950s and 1960s. Meg Greenfield, editorial page editor of the *Washington Post* in the 1970s, put this well in her memoir:

> We, especially some of us in the journalism business, were much too gullible and complaisant in the old days. Just as a matter of republican principle, the hushed, reverential behavior (Quiet! Policy is being made here!) had gotten out of hand. It encouraged public servants to believe that they could get away with anything – and they did.[36]

The news media seem to have hit their stride – or a plateau – of acceptance in American life in the 1950s and 1960s, an era in which journalists could be powerful, prosperous, independent, disinterested, public-spirited, trusted, and even occasionally adored by the powerful and the ordinary citizen alike. It was sustained by a bipartisan Cold War political consensus and by the growing economic prosperity of news organizations. Neither would last, nor would the easy assumption that journalism could be simultaneously part of a governing establishment and independent from it. And the beginning of the end of that moment was Vietnam. To cite Greenfield again:

> The mystique had decreed that the people in charge in Washington knew best. They could make things happen if they wanted to. Almost all of them were acting in good faith. And they were entitled to both privacy and discretion to do what they judged necessary for the nation's well-being.[37]

Those blithe assumptions, borne on the wings of World War II and the Cold War to follow, crashed in Vietnam. (All that said, it would be a mistake to see the emergence of Objectivity 2.0 and the recognition of the need for interpretation as something that happened, or that can be explained, in exclusively

American terms. Studies show Swedish television news taking on more "critical scrutiny" as it developed in the 1970s and after, Japanese broadcasting becoming less deferential to political elites over time, British television news interviewers becoming more aggressive and critical toward politicians, and print reporters in Brazil, Argentina, and Peru becoming more aggressive and more likely to report scandal over time.)[38]

Objectivity 2.0 rose on the very grounds that would threaten it – a radical suspicion of authority, and it should be no surprise that "question authority," something of a journalistic watchword after the 1960s and "watchdog journalism," a phrase that gained currency only in the 1960s and after, along with "accountability journalism," could be turned back on journalism itself.

Beyond Objectivity 2.0?

Might there be a mode of professionalism yet to come that still embraces some version of a quest for objectivity: an Objectivity 3.0? Or are we at some moment ready to declare that we are beyond objectivity? I am not ready to predict the future. But I do have an inkling of what we should acknowledge about actual journalism as a basis for moving into the future. It is important that journalism not throw out the baby of professionalism with the bath water swirling around us today. User-generated content has shown considerable value, but it is occasional and normally based on happenstance rather than regular deployment. Partisan journalism is also usefully instructive – not partisan scuttlebutt or partisan ranting or ideological tracts or fabrications, but fact-based discursive practices rooted in reporting on questions that one comes to because of a particular partisan set of values.

But the professionalism my colleagues teach at Columbia Journalism School – and that is still taken seriously at hundreds of newsrooms across the country and taught at scores of journalism schools – insists that students learn to report "against their own assumptions." If you believe strongly in "pro-choice" (favoring a "woman's right to choose" an abortion if she so desires) and you are assigned to write about the pro-life movement (which declares abortion to be murder and opposes almost all abortions), and you are charged with understanding the pro-life position and why pro-life advocates believe in it, your task is to represent the position and the people fairly and accurately. If your favorite candidate for the Senate in Connecticut in 2010 was Richard Blumenthal, and he was the favorite of the *New York Times* editorial board, and as the *Times* reporter covering the race you find that Blumenthal has spoken misleadingly about his military service, you report what his military service record shows and how his statements about it misrepresented it. You break that story because it is a good story – it is relevant news to the voters of Connecticut. And of course you talk to Mr. Blumenthal and report his explanation of his language, too. And that is exactly what the *New York Times* did. In 2016 it was the *New York Times*, not Fox News, not *Breitbart News*, that broke the story that Hillary Clinton as Secretary of State used a private server for emails, including confidential State Department communications. *The Times* is a professional Objectivity 2.0 news organization with a staff of dedicated Objectivity 1.0 and Objectivity 2.0 reporters and editors. They follow the story, not their own or their publisher's or their editorial page editor's preferences.

And in 2018 and beyond? Professional journalism still seeks to provide context. It still includes an ethic of inquiry and a determination to hold government power to account – and, in a less organized and less insistent fashion, to hold other power centers, notably corporate power, to account, too. It probably also needs to include being as transparent as is consistent with good reporting – that is, sometimes you will not be able to publicly identify your sources because they would not talk to you without a promise of confidentiality. They may legitimately fear losing their job or, in some reporting situations, they may reasonably fear assault or murder.

The notion that transparency is a good replacement for objectivity as an ideal has been discussed over the past several years, but it seems to me hopelessly wrong-headed. It seems to accept the most cynical view of reporting – that reporters are slaves to their own preconceptions and preferences. If these fixed positions are revealed, the reader or viewer will have all the necessary tools to see – which is to say, to see through – the stories the reporter writes. Anyone who has ever been trained in any physical or mental skill knows better: you can be trained out of bad habits, even deeply ingrained ones. You can be trained – as a painter, as a writer of fiction or nonfiction, as a psychologist, or as a reporter to see what is before your eyes and to act accordingly. I once took a class in "life drawing" where the instructor's regularly repeated mantra was, "Draw what you see." But isn't that just what I was doing? I asked. No, he insisted, you are drawing what you think you *should* see. You are drawing the figure the way your preconceptions have led you to think a figure should be drawn. Look more closely at the model before you and draw what you see. This was not enough to make me a great artist, but my drawings markedly improved.

If an Objectivity 3.0 were to be mostly about transparency, it would presumably call for public disclosure of some aspects of journalists' backgrounds and qualifications, but this would not work without a public understanding that has not been secured – that disclosure is not disqualification. Can reporters cover controversial Facebook policies if they are not on Facebook? Would it be worse if they *are* on Facebook? Can you cover the auto industry in Detroit if you drive a Japanese car? Would that bias you in a way to disqualify you? Or would it be driving a Detroit-made car that would bias you? Can a Jew or a Mormon cover news of the Pope? What about an atheist? Can a man cover a story about abortion fairly? Or a woman who has had an abortion? Or a woman who has not? Should the reporter assigned to a story on the pro-life or pro-choice movement reveal the experience of and attitudes toward abortion of close friends and family whose views influence his or her own?

These are not frivolous questions in a time of identity politics, but they will not move anyone toward full disclosure as a new standard for a professional ethic in journalism. I think journalism is stuck with straddling an abyss between binding itself in a straitjacket of "nothing but the facts" and a premise of sensible interpretive and contextual reporting that stops well short of partisan advocacy. Others may see around the corner on this topic but so far I do not. Transparency as a political ideal cannot repeal or replace objectivity.

What I do see is that Objectivity 1.0 – due regard for fact-based reporting – is part of what journalists do. But Objectivity

1.0 denies another part of what journalists do – they do not just report facts, they also write stories. Objectivity 2.0 accepts the need to structure reports so that the audience is equipped with sufficient context and analysis to comprehend them. Sometimes this may subordinate the central necessity of the factual reporting, but it does not bury it. Objectivity 3.0, if it is to emerge, must acknowledge both the requirements of reporting and the needs of telling a comprehensible story. I cannot picture a form that remains reliably professional that does not insist that journalism be "evidence-based" at heart. Nor is it easy to imagine shearing off the advances that analysis and investigation, as emphasized in Objectivity 2.0, have contributed. What I can imagine is an Objectivity 3.0 that might add to this an objectivity of empathy.

What I mean by this is straightforward. Think of the contradiction at the heart of what physicians do. Doctors are both people who are trained in the sciences and people who are trained to be healers. They follow practices dictated by science and at the same time they engage in practices based on the unique persons who present themselves as patients. The genius of great doctors (or so it seems to me) is that they do both at once without denying either. Their knowledge is both schooled and clinical. They live off of both textbooks and techniques they can articulate and clinical judgment that no algorithm has yet captured. A doctor who denied one side of the healing task or the other would be denying a part of himself or herself.

Similarly, journalism practiced with Objectivity 3.0 should accept that the job of journalism is to report stories about contemporary life. By reporting, journalists make a commitment to a factual and, to a large extent, verifiable world. By turning those reports into stories, journalists give their reporting a form that makes them understandable, even compelling. Reports in story form have a point. They are not just transcripts. They are a combination of reportage and story that not only informs and instructs but may touch people, even move them. And to do that, the reporters must seek to place themselves in the positions of the people they write about. This is not a matter of sentimentality but of a further depth in standing aside from one's own standpoint. True, a woman who has had an abortion and regrets it cannot leave that experience fully behind in reporting on a pro-life or a pro-choice rally. Another woman who has had an abortion and feels it was a well-considered and good decision cannot leave her experience fully behind either. But both may be able to bracket their own standpoints in the quest to get at someone else's. People do not always succeed at such a balancing act, but we attempt it with some frequency. A parent advising a child, a teacher counseling a student, a nurse a patient, a friend a friend are all capable of saying, "Let me try to put myself in your shoes. ..." That is an act of empathic objectivity – and what that might mean in journalism in an era in which we are so strongly encouraged to express ourselves is worth considering. Objectivity 3.0 is a discipline of not expressing, of setting self-expression temporarily aside. It is a form of tact, and tact is a form of empathy.

The next moment in journalism ethics is not transparency or disclosure but the full acceptance that journalism is "reporting stories" and that the complexity of that apparently simple phrase is one that journalists must accommodate the best they can. Reporting without the story achieves only part of the aim. A story without reporting is unconvincing, or fanciful, or a lie. Like the doctor who must keep both science and patient in view, the reporter has an impossibly difficult task that can never be flawlessly completed, but when it is well executed, it can be eye-opening, it can hold power to account in ways no other institution in society does with such public exposure, and it thereby can be the source of great public good. And all this is normally undertaken not to achieve a specific political goal but to serve the larger aims of a vocation that holds that the fair-minded pursuit of truth, even truths uncomfortable or inconvenient, is the greatest service journalism can offer society.

Part II

Going Deeper into Contemporary Journalism

4

The Danger of Independent Journalism

This is the oldest paper in this book, published originally in 2005 in Rodney Benson and Erik Neveu's co-edited *Bourdieu and the Journalistic Field* (Polity). I think it remains a clarifying corrective to views that offer unqualified praise of journalistic independence, so I have revived it here with a few modest changes in the text that help pull it into the present moment.

The late Pierre Bourdieu, the single most influential French sociologist of the past half century, introduced the concept of "field" to provide a vocabulary and framework for understanding how different realms of social life are related to one another while remaining distinct from one another, each field having some measure of autonomy and therefore needing to be understood to some degree on its own terms. Bourdieu observes not only that each social field has its own logic, but that some fields are more independent in their logics than others. He cites poetry and mathematics as fields where internal logic is relatively more determining than relationships to external social, economic, and political phenomena.

With respect to journalism as a field, Bourdieu's work led his students to many studies that examine how independent journalism is from other fields that have tried to bring journalism into their own orbits. In other terms, this has been a perennial concern of both journalism's critics and its defenders: how can a news operation keep itself from being colonized by its own business objectives, thereby losing much of its autonomy vis-à-vis the economic field, the market? Or, in other settings, how can journalism keep from being compromised by subservience to the political field and the force of the state?

What has not been given very much serious consideration in these discussions is whether the ideal world is one of complete independence of the journalistic field from other fields. The assumption is strong inside journalism and in most academic and popular discussions of journalism that the press should be fully autonomous, pursuing truth without constraint and "without fear or favor," as the publisher of the *New York Times* wrote in 1896. But from the perspective of democratic theory, just how autonomous should journalism really be?

In practice, journalistic autonomy is complex. Consider Daniel Hallin's classic 1986 study of American news coverage of the war in Vietnam. Hallin observes that press subservience to government officials and press acquiescence in an ideology of the Cold War muted criticism of the evolving Vietnam policy of the Kennedy and Johnson administrations. Criticism was muted – but not silenced; the journalistic field was under the influence of the political field, but not entirely so. The television networks were more submissive than print. Print was more acquiescent in its headlines than in its news stories. Print news was more docile in front-page stories than in those on the inside pages. Front-page stories were more cautious in their leads and opening paragraphs than in the closing paragraphs. Reporters typically led with recent and authoritative views of highly placed government officials, but the further one read into the story, the more the reporters included policy discussions and details that cut closer to the heart of where the policies were going and what they portended. Hallin wrote of one story that it "led with the statement least revealing of the actual course of the policy debate, and moved on, as coverage trailed off into the back pages, to information that progressively undermined the lead – and moved closer to the truth."[1]

For Hallin, the American press in the 1960s was by no means independent of state power. Although Hallin acknowl-

edges that US journalism had become increasingly professionalized and dominated by its own occupational routines
and its own professional ethic, he insists that it is wrong to
describe this as the differentiation between an autonomous
sphere of journalism and an earlier incorporation inside the
state. He put it this way:

> Far from sundering the connection between press and state,
> objective journalism *rationalized* that connection, in the Webe-
> rian sense of the term: it put that relation on a firm footing
> of a set of abstract principles embodied in the "professional"
> standards of news judgment. It was no longer possible for a
> party or politician to control any news medium as an official
> organ; and it was no longer necessary for high officials of
> government to do so. Their views were guaranteed access to
> all the major media – and protected against "irresponsible"
> attack – by virtue of the authority of their position, not their
> particular party or politics.[2]

The press, in Hallin's view, did not live up to its ambition – or
boast – of serving as a "watchdog" on government. The media
were far too integrated into the political field or, in Hallin's
terms rather than Bourdieu's, the media's relationship to politics had become rationalized in a way that privileged official
government voices in the news. Nevertheless, within a single
news institution and even within a single news story in that
institution, variations in the degree of subordination to the
state are apparent.

Press reports on politics, W. Lance Bennett has argued, are
"indexed" to the views of high government officials.[3] Hallin's
work, among many others, confirms this for the United States.
Eric Darras illustrates the same point for France in a study
of French television news interview programs. He finds that
these programs select guests largely according to the ranking
of the individuals within the political elite. One can imagine
alternative possibilities – that journalists choose guests who
will broaden the political debates or guests whose personali-
ties and rhetoric might entice a larger audience and so prove
commercially more attractive – but neither of these imaginable
possibilities fit the data.[4]

Bourdieu himself suggested that journalists construct a sense
of their own autonomy "against the commercial." In the

American case, this is a matter of routine discussion among journalists where the separation of the news department from the "business side" responsible for selling subscriptions and selling advertising space has been referred to as "the separation of church and state," suggesting by loose analogy that it is foundational or constitutional in protecting the legitimate mission of independent news-gathering. There is a century-long tradition in the US of journalistic fears of ceding occupational freedom of action to pressure from advertisers or directives from profit-seeking publishers. In the 1990s it was a national scandal when the *Los Angeles Times* ran as "news" a supplement about the city's new convention and sports center that was actually a large paid advertisement. What was scandalous then has since become common practice under the alias of "native advertising," essentially the same thing but with the fig leaf of an inconspicuous notice that the piece the reader has just read, written to mimic a news story, is actually a paid advertisement.

For American journalists, autonomy is constructed against the economic field but also against the political field, and they police the possibility of acquiescence to political power with an even greater sense of moral indignation over violations. The First Amendment is the backbone of American journalism's understanding of itself, even though the First Amendment's prohibition on government laws abridging freedom of the press had essentially no significance in the courtroom until the 1920s. Moreover, the First Amendment has sometimes been read by the courts and used by news organizations to identify press freedom or journalistic autonomy with the inviolable right of media owners to publish as they please. Consider the case of Pat Tornillo, who ran for a seat in the Florida state legislature in 1972. The *Miami Herald*, the most influential newspaper in Florida, wrote some scathing editorials about him. Tornillo asked for space in the paper to respond, citing a 1913 Florida "right-of-reply" statute that required newspapers to provide comparable space for reply, upon request, should a newspaper assail the personal character of a candidate for public office. When the *Miami Herald* refused to satisfy Tornillo's request, he sued. The Florida Supreme Court held that the right-of-reply statute served the "broad societal interest in the free flow of information to the public."

Most democracies around the world would agree with the ruling. Right-of-reply statutes are commonplace and obviously consistent with a general norm of fairness. But the US Supreme Court overruled the Florida Court. Supreme Court Justice Byron White saw in Florida's statute "the heavy hand of government intrusion" that would make the government "the censor of what people may read and know." For Justice White, if the marketplace is to be the censor, that may be regrettable, but it does not violate the Constitution. It is only state censorship that the Constitution forbids.[5]

Although the character of journalistic autonomy varies from one country to another, journalists around the world who have accepted the importance of fostering independent news judgment struggle against subservience to the state and to the market. But suppose that they were entirely successful and gained complete independence from the commercial field and the political field. Would they then have achieved autonomy? Bourdieu makes a shrewd observation that is the touchstone for the rest of this essay: "Autonomy can lead to an 'egoistic' closing-in on the specific interests of the people engaged in the field."[6] This restates in Bourdieu's theoretical terms a practical political complaint that conservatives have routinely made in the US of the mainstream media – that it has been captured by journalists themselves. They see journalists as a liberal elite that imposes its values on everybody else. Journalists seek to be "politically correct." They are almost uniformly secular in a country with the strongest church-going tradition of any democracy in Europe or North America. Journalists are feminists and pro-choice advocates when a very large and politically powerful segment of the population is deeply distressed by abortion laws that they consider to be too permissive.

The conservative charges have been widely circulated at least since the 1960s and they have been famously if crudely renewed by President Donald Trump. Even the older versions of the charges have typically been extreme. Conservative critics have failed to understand how wedded to the dominant political dialogue – to "indexing" – the news media are. They fail to understand how seriously journalists salute the flag of objectivity. Even so, there is a socially liberal, if not politically liberal, tone to the leading institutions of American journalism (although probably not to American journalism top to bottom). How much is journalism's autonomy, so far as it goes, an "egoistic closing-in" that conservatives rightly call out and that others who hope for a fair-minded accounting of politics from leading news organizations should also be concerned about?

In the daily practice of journalism, autonomy is a condition of work that honest editors and reporters seek. They do not want to bow to pressure from government officials, on the one hand, or to media owners, advertisers, and market competition, on the other. They want to be true to their own professional news judgment. Of course, "news judgment" is not in fact "their own" individually, but their own as the collective construction of the journalistic field or the journalistic community. It is not codified. It is not fully coherent. In tough cases, it has to be debated among reporters and editors: "Is this a story? Is it a front-page story? Is the tip or rumor that just came to us worth pursuing?" No formula covers every instance. No two news organizations operate in precisely the same way. Still, journalists all breathe the same air of their occupation and develop habits of judgment of great – sometimes stultifying – uniformity. In this respect, when journalists gain autonomy from state and market, they do not individually gain free expression, but acquire collectively the freedom to be directed exclusively by the values and practices of their own community.

This raises the possibility that full autonomy for media professionals who are beyond the influence of state and market is not necessarily a prize one should want for the best interest of a democratic society. Journalists are right that commercial and government control are corruptions they should strenuously avoid, but the corruption of conformity to a climate of opinion in their own professional peer group can be serious and damaging in its own right. Consider the conformity of opinion in a small quasi-religious cult that expects the end of the world on a predicted day and prepares to welcome the flying saucer that will save them from earth's destruction. When the saucer fails to land and the earth is not destroyed on the anticipated date, the group does not alter its faith in its millenarian vision but seeks to understand why it got the date wrong. Or consider the far more important case of scientific communities in philosopher of science Thomas Kuhn's powerful portrait of them. Kuhn shows that conformity to a reigning scientific framework continues even in the face of a growing array of puzzles that cannot be understood within it. Even when a new and more successful model appears, adherents of the old paradigm do not typically convert – they eventually die off while younger scientists champion the new view.[7]

If journalism were fully autonomous, would it not be subject to corruptions like this? Is journalism, even more than science, unlikely to police its own intellectual narrowness? Journalists collectively do very little to challenge their own governing assumptions. What keeps journalism alive, changing, and growing is the public nature of journalists' work, the non-autonomous environment of their work, the fact that their sources are disappointed or critical of the work they have produced, and, likewise, that their audience registers disappointment or disapproval or boredom by canceling subscriptions, changing channels, or publicly criticizing on Twitter or in online comments on news organizations' own websites. Vulnerability to government and other political sources keeps journalists nimble in one direction; vulnerability to the audience – the market – keeps them on their toes in another. What can be good for journalism can also be disastrous – propagandizing in the political field, and pandering in the economic field to win an audience. But absent these powerful outside pressures, journalism can wind up communicating only to itself and for itself.

What also keeps journalism alive, and what social scientists typically and persistently forget, is its dependence not only on the state and the market, but also on the drama of events that neither state nor market nor journalists can fully or even approximately anticipate or control. Unanticipated events, from assassinations to terrorism to tornados, lie at the center of journalistic passions, but beyond the foresight of established power. The nuclear power plant accident at Three Mile Island, Pennsylvania in 1979 forced American media to pay attention to environmental issues and energy issues and the potential dangers of nuclear power generators in a way that no protest movements or blue-ribbon commissions ever could. Unanticipated events on the scale of Three Mile Island or, even more cataclysmic, September 11 are rare. The White House press corps covers the president as close to round-the-clock as it can, not because the president is so endlessly important or fascinating, but because his assassination or heart attack would be. This may be ghoulish, but it organizes journalistic effort.

Covering a hurricane or flood or murder brings career advancement for individual reporters and may secure major prizes for news organizations. Most news is routine, but the ideology of American journalism focuses insistently on exploits and challenges that arise when routines fail. It is not easy to accommodate this feature of journalism any more than it is easy for historians to know how to make sense of the assassin's bullet in Sarajevo or in Dallas that, through no particular logic, influenced the course of history. But a sociological understanding of journalism has to find a way to do this.

The membrane of the journalistic field, permeable in relation to the market and the state, is relatively resistant to influence from other groups. Young people have occasionally organized to influence how teenagers are portrayed in the news, but they have had an uphill battle.[8] Academic experts who hope their views will be taken seriously in the media are often rudely rebuffed. In the United States, journalists typically seek out only certain kinds of experts to comment on politics – those who are or have been close to government and who are adept at talking the talk of policy options and predictions. Authorities who might want to stand a bit further back from "inside Washington" and offer views on, say, the history of a conflict or the morality of a policy are unlikely to get a hearing from a reporter on deadline.[9]

So what degree of autonomy should one wish for journalism? A democrat should not want journalists to be as self-enclosed and separated from outside pressures as mathematicians or poets. At least in an American view, which I share, journalism is not supposed to be a platform for a set of individual thinkers and explorers in search of truth, but a collective enterprise of energetic, informed, and curious communicators who try to keep a society attuned to itself and its environment. Journalism, as the primary circulator of public meanings in society, the realm in which the ideas and values of other fields and other lands come to the same page before a wide array of readers and viewers, should be dependent to an extent – but an extent difficult to measure – on the market. The market is an imperfect proxy for the general public, but of course there are different markets and market segments and, accordingly, different publics and elements of the public so represented.

Journalists should also be particularly attuned to the state. An argument can be made, in terms of democratic theory, that journalism should be significantly occupied with relaying the views of both elected and appointed government officials as well as aspirants for public office. Who are journalists, after all, to determine what information, what history, and what context is appropriate for citizens who want to be informed about political life? Why should a democracy trust in the intellectual currents and fashions ruling journalists at a particular moment rather than in the dynamics of forces pushing or pulling politicians who have the legitimacy of being popularly elected? Perhaps journalists, consistent with democracy, should concentrate on reporting back to citizens what their elected representatives say and do, allowing citizens as voters to assess leaders after they have acted?[10]

This would narrow the role of political news too much. Journalists should not deny themselves or their audiences the avenues of analysis and criticism. They should be active in opening up the windows of musty political rooms and airing out the public sphere, even when politicians are content to breathe their own fetid air. But at the same time, they can and should give disproportionate space and attention to the people's elected representatives. A degree of deference by journalists to elected legislators and presidents demonstrates some very prosaic democratic virtues – dutifulness, humility, a sense of place and of proportion.

If journalism is sufficiently decentralized and varied in the viewpoints it presents; if journalists are recruited from different walks of life and if they present different perspectives; if journalism is institutionally self-critical in ways that guarantee variety and change in the news; if, in a word, journalistic is pluralistic, then autonomy may be good not only for journalists, who of course appreciate the freedom to write what they please, but good for democracy. Pluralism inside media organizations helps open a space for what sociologist Herbert J. Gans calls "multiperspectival news."[11] Honest observers can disagree over how pluralistic journalism is in one country or another and on how one might measure it. But only if journalism is relatively pluralistic, and only if journalism remains relatively vulnerable to the assaults of government sources, marketplace competition, and the surprises of daily events can we be confident that it will not be captive to an insular professional elite.

These observations raise more questions than they answer. How can journalists, in their search to be free from the threats of the state and the market to their independence not find themselves captured by preferences and prejudices of their own journalistic tribe? What structures of journalistic owner-ship, recruitment, culture, and organization can keep the work of news-gathering open to alternative opinions? Since depend-ence on the state and on the market affords journalism ways for democratic sentiment and democratic values to enter into news production, is it possible to recognize the point at which dependence on the state becomes serfdom and dependence on the market becomes crass exploitation?

In the end, journalistic autonomy should be valued but not for its own sake. Journalism can do many things but one thing it is obliged to do – by its history, its traditions, and its highest aspirations, and sometimes its legal license – is to serve liberal democracy. Autonomy is sought to that end, but when auton-omy conflicts with the best practices of a democratic society, autonomy must be challenged.

5

Belgium Invades Germany: Reclaiming Non-Fake News – Imperfect, Professional, and Democratic

This paper began as a keynote address at a conference on fake news at Boston University in 2017, organized by James E. Katz and the Department of Emerging Media. I revised it for a presentation a couple months later at Raritan Valley Community College and yet again since. It is published now for the first time. In a somewhat different form, it will also appear in a volume that James E. Katz is editing for MIT Press.

Donald Trump: I will mention his name only a few times here, this time just to say he did not invent fretful and bitter relations between truth and politics. Nor did George W. Bush, although his peculiar relationship to truth inspired Stephen Colbert in 2005 to develop the notion of "truthiness." President Bush, Colbert said, accepted as true what "felt" true, what he wanted to be true.

But people have been complaining about false news or fake news for about as long as there have been newspapers. And serious commentary about the truth/politics relationship goes back centuries. One landmark in truth/politics criticism is philosopher Hannah Arendt's simply titled "Truth and Politics." This was published not in a philosophical journal but, just over 50 years ago, in *The New Yorker*.[1] At that time, Donald Trump was in college. Stephen Colbert was three years old. There was no Mark Zuckerberg. But truth and politics were not on good terms.

Arendt's essay is a starting point for understanding how complicated ascertaining the truth is, how difficult it is to assess what is or is not truthful, how dangerous it is that people make things up, and how profoundly troubling it is that lies, as well as truths, now circulate at speeds we can't comprehend and often by agents called "bots" that are lies themselves from top to bottom, online mechanical devices programmed to comment on, praise, attack, forward, retweet, recirculate online items while posing as humans. I will try to connect Arendt's observations specifically to journalism, one of the key truth-seeking institutions of modern societies for roughly the past 100 or 120 years. (See chapter 3 if you believe there has been a particularly close relationship of news institutions to truth before then, or Chapter 7 if you suspect that the economic woes of contemporary journalism mean a contribution of journalism to truth has recently ended.)

Like science, like all human efforts to find the truth, journalism is imperfect. But historically journalism became a professional vocation over the past century and I want to argue that that matters – enormously – to all of us and to the future of a liberal democratic society.

Power, Arendt held, threatens truth, especially "factual truth" rather than formal truths like "two plus two equals four." Factual truth is more vulnerable because "facts and events – the invariable outcome of men living and acting together – constitute the very text of the political realm."[2] But Arendt realized that facts were under assault:

> Do facts independent of opinion and interpretation, exist at all? Have not generations of historians and philosophers of history demonstrated the impossibility of ascertaining facts without interpretation, since they must first be picked out of a chaos of sheer happenings (and the principles of choice are surely not factual data) and then be fitted into a story that can be told only in a certain perspective, which has nothing to do with the original occurrence?[3]

For Arendt, the complexity of sorting out fact from interpretation is not an argument against the existence of facts. She tells a little story, of Georges Clemenceau, prime minister of

France during World War I. A few years after the war, he was discussing the question of which country was responsible for initiating that horrendous, world-shattering, and pointless conflict. Clemenceau was asked what future historians would conclude. He responded, "This I don't know. But I know for certain that they will not say Belgium invaded Germany." Now, if your World War I history is a little rusty, let me remind you that on August 4, 1914, German troops crossed into neutral Belgium. Germans recognized this. Belgians recognized this. Declarations of war had been flying across Europe for a week at that point but this was the opening act of blood-spilling aggression, when the German army attacked Belgium en route to France, the country they were at war with.

Some things, Clemenceau asserts, are just simply facts. And Arendt at first seems to agree, despite having acknowledged the social construction of reality. But then, she backs away. She adds that this fact – German troops moved into Belgium on August 4, 1914 – like any other fact is vulnerable to power. It would take "a power monopoly over the entire civilized world" to erase the recognition that German troops invaded Belgium, not that Belgian troops invaded Germany.

Ahh, then truth is safe? No. Arendt writes that "such a power monopoly is far from being inconceivable, and it is not difficult to imagine what the fate of factual truth would be if power interests, national or social, had the last say in these matters."[4]

Our Imperfect Knowledge

That is my text for this sermon. *Time* Magazine asked on its April 3, 2017 cover, "Is Truth Dead?" (And here, of course, it would not be out of line to mention Donald Trump again, whose casual relationship to truth is unsettling and undeniable.) If truth is dead, it has been dead at least since Arendt's famous essay. But I want to argue that the correct answer to *Time* Magazine's question is "no." Or, following Arendt, no, not so long as "power interests" can be prevented from having the last say. We live in a real world where men and women living and acting together produce facts and events that even the powerful must reckon with. At the April 22, 2017 "March for Science" in Washington, DC, there were signs and t-shirts that read, "I Can't Believe I'm Marching For Facts." I feel similarly. I can't believe that what I want to say is simply that we do not live in a post-truth age and that we never will.

For Arendt, the guarantor of facts is what she calls "viewpoint outside the political realm," or what she also calls "one of the various modes of being alone."[5] People standing alone have the independence to be truth-tellers, and she listed the following categories of truth-telling: "the solitude of the philosopher, the isolation of the scientist and the artist, the impartiality of the historian and the judge, and the independence of the fact-finder, the witness, and the reporter."[6]

This is eloquent, but it is an entirely unrealistic portrait of independent thinkers. There *are* independent truth-tellers. One of them, more stubborn and dogged than most, is David Fahrenthold of the *Washington Post*, who was awarded the 2016 Pulitzer Prize for national reporting for turning over every possible stone to find out whether Donald Trump or his foundation made large contributions to charity as he had claimed (Fahrenthold found no support for Trump's claim and a lot of evidence to contradict it). Fahrenthold is independent-minded, but not a solo practitioner or freelancer. Other journalists have made their contributions with little or no institutional support, like I. F. Stone in the 1950s or Seymour Hersh, who in 1969 uncovered the US massacre at the village of My Lai, Vietnam when he was a freelance reporter with no institutional backing. But most journalists and most historians, most philosophers, and most scientists do not work without salaries and libraries and newsrooms and laboratories and professional associations and peer review and graduate student assistants and a deep array of support systems. It is only with all that help that, normally, they stand independently from the political world.

What conditions must be preserved to permit people to take these standpoints outside the political? And what are the conditions of reality that must be acknowledged that power cannot overcome?

Consider how truth-seeking operates in science. Science, like journalism, is not like Mount Everest. It is not the natural world itself but a human construction about the natural world.

It is much more like Mount Rushmore – it is made from natural materials but it is made by humans working together. And are its conclusions absolutely true? Certainly not. After all, they change quite often. They change for science and scientists. They may change because some new information turns up that invalidates the old information. They may also change because the framework assumptions or "paradigms" that guide scientists about what data to look at and what questions to ask change. And how does this happen? How does one paradigm replace another? Atomic physicist Max Planck gave a simple and distressing answer: they change because an older generation committed to the old paradigm dies out and a new generation rises to power: "A new scientific truth does not triumph by convincing its opponents and making them see the light, but rather because its opponents eventually die, and a new generation grows up that is familiar with it."[7] Science advances, as Planck is supposed to have said, "one funeral at a time."

Truth is a set of agreements. It is a social consensus. But that does not mean the consensus is unconstrained by conditions of reality. The distinguishing feature of the agreements we think of as "truth" is that they correspond to what we know or think we know about an external world. There are realities that act as a brake on consensus gone wild. You may or may not believe your life is one moment in a cycle of rebirths. But you will not disagree with my proposition that in this part of the cycle you were born from the womb of a woman. No exceptions. You do not know when or how you will die, but you are 100 percent confident, as am I, that, in this moment of your eternal cycle, if that is your belief, or in your only lifetime on earth, if that is your belief, you will die. No exceptions. Reality does not necessarily limit our imaginations or our wishes, but it constrains our theorizing about what is so. We cannot posit as true just any propositions that please us.

A poignant and comic sign held up by a child at the San Francisco Women's March in January, 2017 (and visible again many times over in the April 2017 March for Science) read as follows: "What do we want? Evidence-based science. When do we want it? After peer review." Indeed. That is how science works. That is what science is: a community of scientists who collectively determine what passes as evidence-based. Arendt's concept of science as one of the various modes of being alone is less true than the recognition that science is a distinctive mode of being together. This community falters when scientists make up their data, and we know that scientific fraud happens. We know that journalistic fraud happens, too. It has happened in recent memory at both the *New York Times* (reporter Jayson Blair was forced to resign in 2003 for plagiarism and fabrication) and *The New Republic* (Stephen Glass was fired in 1998 for fabricating all or parts of most of his published work in the magazine). These were not cases of bias, but of total fabrication. Science, too, is vulnerable to total fabrication.

In everyday life, people past and present readily believe exaggerations and lies and even wild fabrications. That is why scam artists, confidence men, rip-off artists who prey on the elderly, Wells Fargo bank executives who invent financial products to defraud their own customers, and mortgage brokers who sell people homes they know their clients will quickly lose all abide with us. The facts constrain, but people believe what they wish to, what accords with preconceptions, what flatters the communities they identify with, what pleases the state that governs them, and what helps explain and assuage their fears, or gives them hopes where reason and experience counsel that there is no hope.

Truth has formidable enemies. It suffers under an onslaught from what we may call the four P's: (1) propaganda – propositions that states promote to gain or extend power; (2) profit – propositions that individuals or organizations circulate to sell products, services, or false hopes in order to make money; (3) prejudices – pre-judgments that many individuals routinely place ahead of actually seeking truth; and (4) pranks – propositions or practices designed to mislead for the sake of a sick joke.

Let me just add that we should not discount pranks as a factor, least of all in an era of fake news. In 2001, while I served as acting provost of the University of California, San Diego's Thurgood Marshall College, one of a handful of undergraduate units of the university, I received a package addressed to the Thurgood Marshall College provost. The college office staff and I learned upon opening it that it contained nothing except a small plastic baggie full of white powder. Similar packages with white powder had been sent in the weeks after 9/11 to several news outlets and sickened some 20 people and killed several of them because the powder was deadly anthrax. We handed the package over to campus police, the police handed it over to haz-mat personnel, and haz-mat took it to the FBI who promptly discarded it without examining it. Why examine it? It was almost surely talcum powder, not anthrax, because hundreds of similar packages had been mailed all over the country – a sick joke indeed. In this case, it was likely also a sick racist joke, since Thurgood Marshall College, named after the first African American justice of the Supreme Court, was the only administrative unit at the university to be targeted.

People will fall prey to untruths because they know no better, because their knowledge is limited, because they do not think through how ridiculously unlikely it is that Pope Francis endorsed Donald Trump for president (or any other candidate, for that matter) or that high-level Democratic Party officials and aides to Hillary Clinton were key figures in a child pornography and satanic ritual conspiracy operating out of the Comet Pizza chain of pizza parlors. But people's divorce from reality need not be large and they may be led to give credit to ridiculous claims for no greater reason than not wanting to appear a fool. Remember the story of the emperor's new clothes, published by Hans Christian Andersen in 1837. It is difficult for most of us to stand alone, even when the penalty for dissent is trivial, and even when our eyes tell us that the king is parading down the street naked.

How do we know what's true? We are no more in a post-truth era than Hans Christian Andersen was 180 years ago, but the conditions under which we learn and can confirm truths have grown complicated in ways we have not yet socially and politically assimilated. Knowing the truth is harder because propaganda, profits, prejudices, and pranks travel more quickly and are empowered by new means of cloaking themselves in the garb of truthfulness. Keeping tabs on the truth has indeed become more difficult today at the same time and by the same mechanism that makes locating truth less difficult than ever – the speed, power, and global reach of online communications.

Philosopher Michael Patrick Lynch has argued that we have today a whole new way of knowing he calls "Google-knowing" and that he defines simply as "knowledge acquired online." And he holds that "Most knowing now is Google-knowing."[8] He contrasts this to experiential knowledge, that is, knowledge derived by "being receptive to the facts outside of ourselves." He also writes of this latter form of knowing as knowledge anchored "by the objective world itself."[9]

Lynch is right that there is something fresh in the world that we rely on and, indeed, rely too much on, that we can call Google-knowledge. It is in many ways transformative. Still, even with Google-knowing, a great deal of our knowledge remains experiential and something that even a unified power structure cannot talk us out of. If I am tortured, can I be convinced by the torturer that it does not hurt? If I feel a sudden, severe pain in my chest, can I be persuaded that I should not call 911? If a woman is in labor, can anything convince her she is not giving birth? These are the powerful realities of bodily experience. There is also memory of bodily experience. In 2017, I gave a talk at Raritan Valley Community College. I was instructed to get there from New York City on a New Jersey Transit train. But how did I know how to find New Jersey Transit in New York? By having used it before. And it turns out that you can buy tickets for NJT's trains at exactly the same place that, as I remembered, I had bought them a year before when I had last traveled on NJT. Experiential knowledge gets stored, more or less accurately, in memory.

That is experiential knowledge. There is also a kind of mediated experiential knowledge people routinely depend on. I may be misled by books or by Google or by news in the news media, but I believe that the news provided by the *New York Times* that I read today is produced by people with roughly the same set of standards as the *New York Times* I have been reading for decades. It has not been perfect. It has admitted to errors and corrected them. It has considered and sometimes accepted public criticism, notably in its "public editor" column, sadly discontinued in 2017. But it has been broadly, in my experience, reliable. We have friends and acquaintances we know from past experience who are very reliable in relating a story or giving directions or recalling who said what when – and there are others we have learned are quite unreliable, even if we love them. We judge – perhaps with more difficulty – news outlets similarly.

Pain, experience, the memory of one's own experience, and the mediated experience we may summarize in the term "reputation" are all agents of provisional verification. None of them perfectly ascertains truthful knowledge but all of them are powerful. A fifth power, and one that underlies the others, is skepticism. We should know that finding truth is complicated, not simple; that it is a cumulative, social activity, not a flash of inspiration even if it incorporates flashes of inspiration; and that it requires vigilant bullshit-detection. Knowledge is not reducible to facts. Half a century ago, historian Richard Hofstadter wrote about conspiracy-minded thinkers and noted that they typically do not ignore facts. They typically are obsessed with facts. What is distinctive is that they marshal their facts toward an overwhelming "proof" of the conspiracy they mean to confirm. "It is nothing if not coherent," Hofstadter writes, "in fact the paranoid mentality is far more coherent than the real world, since it leaves no room for mistakes, failures, or ambiguities." It is not that the conspiracy-minded have no facts, but that they use them as scaffolding toward a "curious leap in imagination that is always made at some critical point in the recital of events." They make a "big leap from the undeniable to the unbelievable."[10] We must have trust in our experience, trust in our bodies, trust in reputations established over time, and skepticism about explanations too good and too coherent to be true.

Professional Journalism

The first newspaper, as far as we know, was published in Strasbourg, Germany in 1605. The first English-language newspaper was published in Amsterdam in 1620. The first newspaper in the American colonies (apart from one in 1690 that survived for only a single issue) was published in 1704 – the Pilgrims who settled in what became Massachusetts apparently survived the cold New England winters without any locally printed news media at all. And for the most part there would be no local news in colonial newspapers until around the 1750s. Most news read by Americans when Benjamin Franklin first started publishing the *Pennsylvania Gazette* in 1729 concerned European political and economic affairs.

From the latter part of the eighteenth century on, newspapers in England and in the American colonies expressed criticism of politicians and accused politicians of lying, or worse. But this was easily discounted because the large majority of newspapers from that point into the first half of the twentieth century were partisan newspapers. The Democratic papers believed the Whig (and later the Republican) presidents and governors and mayors were liars; the Whig, and later the Republican, papers thought that only the Democratic presidents and governors and mayors lied.

How that changed is a long story told elsewhere.[11] It is a story of journalism becoming a self-conscious and proud occupational group relatively – not fully, but relatively – independent of the views and values of the newspaper publisher. Once publishers figured out that they could make a lot of money running a newspaper, they began to care less about whether news stories favored one political side or another and to care more about whether news stories attracted readers. If the news could attract readers, newspaper circulation could attract advertisers, and the publisher could get rich. This commercialization of the press provided relative freedom for the reporters to write independent-minded news.

Independent-minded news could attract criticism from left and right. How do you guard against that? You write down the middle. Lyndon Johnson is said to have told a story about a man applying for a position teaching science in a public school in rural Texas in the midst of the depression. The school board interviewed him. He seemed to be doing well at the interview and then one board member said, "Mr. Jones, do you believe the world is flat or the world is round?" Mr. Jones looked at the board members and, not seeing a clue on their faces, replied, "I reckon I can teach it either way." And for a long time, journalists behaved similarly. He said, she said. Report, don't judge.

Despite 300 years of journalism history, a fact-checking movement in journalism has been formally organized only since the early 2000s, beginning with Factcheck.org in 2003.[12] And fact-checking has been made possible by two relatively new features in journalism. The first was the rise of investigative reporting, contextual and critical reporting. In a variety of studies of US journalism and Swedish public broadcasting and German and French and Dutch news media over time, it is clear that the 1960s and 1970s were tantamount to a watershed era that brought a new skepticism and critical instinct to journalism – as Chapter 3 details. The most misleading word in all of US journalism history is "muckraking," because it makes us believe that we have had a strong tradition of fearless investigative work in journalism since the days of Teddy Roosevelt. But the muckrakers criticized by Teddy Roosevelt produced their work for a handful of new middle-class magazines and the vogue for muckraking lasted not quite a decade and it never spread into the general circulation daily newspapers responsible for the lion's share of reporting and reaching by far the largest number of readers.

The second factor that made fact-checking organizations possible is Google-knowing. True, fact-checkers do not rely exclusively on Google-knowledge. They also interview experts. They also examine documents (although often they find these documents through links on Google). And then they try to make judgments about whether politicians' assertions are fact or fiction. We know that nonsense and bullshit and lies circulate rapidly online. We all know people who say without blushing that the source of their knowledge about this or that is "the internet." That's not an answer. "Facebook" is not an answer. "The newspaper" is not an answer. But "Wikipedia" is an answer. *The New York Times* is an answer. "Fox News" is an answer. These are all news institutions, very different ones, with enough of a track record to give us enough context to approximate how and how much to believe what they report.

There is a playfulness in how the fact-checking organizations that emerged in the United States (and now in many other countries) have presented themselves. On the one hand, the whole project is very serious, rooted in a belief that one can stand outside politics, that facts exist, and that facts in the end matter. On the other hand, fact checkers recognize a certain comedy in their exercise and so they present their work in a self-mocking vein. The *Washington Post* FactChecker does not make a binary judgment between true and false, but awards from one to four "Pinocchios" for the degree to which a politician's assertion strays from solid truth. Or take Politifact's measurement of five degrees of factuality from "True" to "Pants on Fire." Its signature symbol is the Truth-O-Meter, a machine for judging the truth of assertions whose chief feature is, of course, that it does not exist. There is no way around the realization that the journalists at fact-checking organizations make consensual judgments among themselves that they expect others to take as honest and fact-based and as authoritative as they know how to make them, even when they themselves know that their authority is more than a little fuzzy around the edges.

What my Columbia Journalism School colleagues tell their students, as I understand it, emphasizes at least three rules that should govern what reporters do. First, be accurate. There's no room for relativism here. The name is either Smith or Jones. The address is either 10 Main Street or 20 Main Street. Taking the average and reporting it as 15 Main Street won't do.

Second, report against your own assumptions. Don't deny that you have views and values and preconceptions. But know what they are and in your reporting look for what might invalidate them and include this in what you write.

Third, follow the story. Even if you find out things that contradict the preferences of you, your publisher, your editor, or the general set of preconceptions in your newsroom, follow wherever the story takes you. The *New York Times* regularly endorsed former Governor Eliot Spitzer for office. But in 2006 it also ran the story about his relations with prostitutes that forced him to resign. No one told the reporter to abandon a story sure to embarrass this potential presidential candidate whom the *New York Times* editorial board admired. The reporter was told to follow the story wherever it would lead. In 2016 *The Times* broke the story of Hillary Clinton's use of a private server for State Department communications while she was Secretary of State. *The Times* endorsed Clinton on the editorial page, but the news story about her email practices may have been more damaging to her chances of being elected than any other news item of the campaign.

That's what it means to be a professional journalist in a professional news organization: it requires a mastery of professional practices and professional ideals that place truth-seeking and truth-telling above profit, above partisanship, above chummy getting-along-with politicians and other powerful groups and individuals. Obviously, it is not always achieved. What is particularly distressing today in the wild territory of the internet is how regularly it is abandoned altogether and scorned.

Democracy as a Skeptical Epistemology

Given enough resources and enough effort, Belgium invaded Germany.

The chance that people will accept that Belgium invaded Germany is greatly enhanced when the most powerful force for persuasion in the world – the views of the President of the United States – are indifferent to or even fiercely hostile to truth if it does not flatter him. Google is powerful. Facebook is powerful. But neither has the power to dominate the public agenda the way American presidents have been doing at least since FDR's fireside chats.

When President Trump went from circulating lies with no sense of obligation to check them out first, to accusing the mainstream media of publishing fake news and being the enemies of the people, he turned "fake news" into some kind of schoolyard taunt.

Democracy is not the best system of government because it puts faith in ordinary people but because it puts faith in no one. C. S. Lewis wrote in the midst of World War II that he was a democrat because, as he put it:

> I believe in the Fall of Man. I think most people are democrats for the opposite reason. A great deal of democratic enthusiasm descends from the ideas of people ... who believed in a democracy because they thought mankind so wise and good that everyone deserved a share in the government. The danger of defending democracy on those grounds is that they're not true. ... The real reason for democracy is ... Mankind is so fallen that no man can be trusted with unchecked power over his fellows.

E. M. Forster said the same thing this way – he offered two cheers for democracy: "One because it admits variety and two because it permits criticism. Two cheers are quite enough: there is no occasion to give three."[13] We can add that democracy, operating as it should, does not just permit criticism but encourages it, nurtures it, requires it.

The American founding fathers were very close to these views. They did not believe that the human species is wise and good. They did not even think they were establishing a "democracy," which meant to them mob rule open to exploitation by demagogues. They were establishing republican government in which white men who owned property would vote for the accepted social leaders of their communities. And they would serve in a government where one branch could prevent another branch from exercising its will, even during a short term of office. The people should be involved, yes, and over time it would come to include men without property, and then men who were not white, and then women, too. America became democratic; it was not born democratic. But Americans inherited from the country's founders a fear of unchecked power, a respect for deliberation, and institutionalized opportunites for revision, repeal, and constant criticism. And this is exactly where the news media come in.

It is a hard lesson to learn – that reality is socially constructed, and that facts are hard to hold steadily in view when we approach them through paradigms and perspectives and prior knowledge and prior ignorance and prior interpretations and presuppositions as we all, always, inevitably do. And – this is the important "and" – at the same time: we can nonetheless affirm that facts exist. Some facts can and will be knocked off their pedestals but, unless truth-seeking is crushed by the weight of power, the facts can be disposed of only by the legitimate array of evidence and reasoning of the sort we would willingly credit as they are employed by the physicians, meteorologists, air traffic controllers, engineers, and a variety of other evidence-reliant classes of people we daily entrust with the task of putting facts above wishes and dreams. Few of us doubt that our lives depend on this. They do – and that is why we do not live in, and in all likelihood will not in the future live in, a "post-truth" era.

Yes, truth is arrived at by social consensus. Yes, our grasp of facts is often shaky as we approach them through various prisms. But the conclusion is not that we live without reliable truths. The conclusion is not that our senses routinely betray us. We know that they normally get us safely across the street.

The American Academy of Arts and Sciences convened a symposium in May, 2017 on "Communicating Science in an Age of Disbelief in Experts." Then one panelist after another disavowed the premise. The convener himself noted that public opinion data showed that Americans tend to hold science and scientists in high regard. The president of the Association of American Universities admitted that she was "not sure that we really are in a new age of disbelief." The former CEO of the American Association for the Advancement of Science agreed and said he doubted "that we are in a special age of disbelief." The science journalist on the panel affirmed that "we are not living in an age of disbelief in experts." And the convener, after everyone's opening remarks, apologized for the program's title, noting sheepishly that "we wanted a title that would grab people's attention."[14]

Facts may be frail and the constitution of them depends on all of the usual and some of the heroic efforts of imperfect human action. This does not mean there are no facts or no science or no expertise. I can't believe that I am marching here for facts, but I do not think there is any other choice.

6

Journalism in a Journalized Society: Reflections on Raymond Williams and the "Dramatised Society"

This chapter is published for the first time here. It is intended as a tribute to Raymond Williams, a scholar I never met but whose work influenced my own. It is a tribute, too, to the Department of Communication at the University of California, San Diego, where I taught from 1981 to 2009. In particular, it is a thank-you note to one of the founding members of that department, Helene Keyssar, a scholar of feminist theater, a dear colleague and friend, who died of cancer in 2001. Among her gifts to me and to that fine department was introducing us to Williams's "Drama in a Dramatised Society."

In 1974, the distinguished scholar Raymond Williams presented "Drama in a Dramatised Society" as his inaugural lecture as Professor of Drama at the University of Cambridge.[1] Williams delivered the main points of his lecture in an allusive style, embracing more the questions than the particular answers about the role of drama in society at that historical moment. He was thinking out loud about the character of a society at least quantitatively more "dramatized" than ever before and perhaps, as he suggested, defined by and named by this feature. This all served a general argument that drama and society are mutually and inevitably related, and at no point in history more so than at that moment.

What occasions my essay in this volume more than 40 years later is that some of Williams's main propositions about drama in 1974 can be applied nearly word for word to journalism in 2018 – as if they were forecasts. That, in itself, should give pause. It is implicitly a pronouncement that the heart of journalism's shifting character today may be less a matter of manifest technological departures than of cultural continuities with the 1960s. Five propositions in Williams's remarkable lecture seem to me especially compelling when we look at them with journalism, not drama, in view.

First, there is a rapid multiplication of dramatic forms.

> Drama is no longer…coextensive with theatre; most dramatic performances are now in film and television studios. In the theatre itself – national theatre or street theatre – there is an exceptional variety of intention and method. New kinds of text, new kinds of notation, new media and new conventions press actively alongside the texts and conventions that we think we know, but that I find problematic just because these others are there.[2]

"Just because these others are there" – I will return to the significance of this simple, potent phrase. For now, note only that Williams is making the claim that drama exists in 1974 in a wide variety of forms, no longer limited to those that for several centuries were performed live on a proscenium stage.

Second, drama has been built into everyday life.

> [I]n our own century, in cinema, in radio and in television…the audience for drama has gone through a qualitative change…for the first time a majority of the population has regular and constant access to drama, beyond occasion and season. But what is really new – so new that it is difficult to see its significance – is that it is not just a matter of audiences for particular plays. It is that drama, in quite new ways, is built into the rhythms of everyday life.[3]

Third, the line between participant and spectator of drama has dissolved.

> Actions of a kind and scale that attract dramatic comparisons are being played out in ways that leave us continually uncertain whether we are spectators or participants. The specific vocabu-

lary of the dramatic mode – drama itself, and then tragedy, scenario, situation, actors, performances, roles, images – is continually and conventionally appropriated for these immense actions.[4]

In short, Williams argued, large majorities of the population have gained regular and constant access to drama and that in some or many of these dramatic performance there was no longer a clear dividing line between spectator and performer.

Fourth, because society grows increasingly complex, it becomes more necessary to see it through dramatic representations (and, implicitly, complexity makes all representations less satisfying).

> We are all used to saying – and it still means something – that we live in a society which is at once more mobile and more complex, and therefore, in some crucial respects, relatively more unknowable, relatively more opaque than most societies of the past, and yet which is also more insistently pressing, penetrating, and even determining.[5]

To put in my own words what I think Williams meant, as society has grown more mobile and more complex, it has become more unknowable. At the same time, it has become more ever-present in people's everyday lives. More than ever before, people are in need of comprehensible representations of the wider social world to help them find their way in it.

Fifth, despite all these changes, people still live their lives primarily at a local, bodily, familial, and familiar level, and this is the context in which social change is experienced and must be understood.

> Yet our lives are still here, still substantially here, with the people we know, in our own rooms, in the similar rooms of our friends and neighbours, and they too are watching: not only for public events, or for distraction, but from a need for images, for representations, of what living is now like, for this kind of person and that, in this situation and place and that.[6]

This one long sentence makes two important points. First, people live their lives, despite all, primarily at a local, face-to-face level, no matter how closely they are connected to a wider world through public media, national political identification, national military service, public schooling, world religions, transnational languages, a global economy, gripping national and global media events, and other forces. Second, the intimacy of everyday life and everyday personal communication is incomplete without efforts to represent the everyday and the efforts of ordinary people to respond to the representations, evaluating them and incorporating their own assessments of them into their lives.

These five propositions from Williams seem to vibrate with meaning for journalism in society today. I think they can help us make sense of journalism today as they did drama just a bit before yesterday. What can we see and what can we say about the place of journalism in a journalized society?

Unjournalized Society

It makes sense to see contemporary society as one that has been "journalized" – and this at a time when "journalism" seems to have become unbound or unhinged and unusually threatened by non-journalisms and anti-journalisms – only if society had been at some earlier point not journalized. Was there ever an unjournalized society? Yes. Before wire services and before 24-hour news linked news organizations. Before dailies. Before extras. Before radio bulletins. Before 24-hour television news. Before all-news radio. Before digital. Before the instantaneity and universality of networked news pickup. Before Facebook and Google and Twitter.

There were newspapers in many parts of the world by 1750, but they were small, rare, and published no more frequently than once a week. There were no wire services (or wires or wireless) and not yet a distinctively journalistic occupation, or a journalistic set of values or self-consciousness or self-organization, or in the existing newspapers a distinctively journalistic voice. In that respect, we have lived in a world unjournalized enough to be journalizable only since some point in the middle of the nineteenth century. The advance of journalism by roughly 1890 was substantial enough to see society then as journalizing in most industrializing countries, although varying by as much as 50 or 75 years from one country to another. Societies began to be attentive to news through journalism, and those producing journalism became self-conscious of their roles in an occupation and of their place in an industry of organizations and people dedicated full-time to news-gathering and news-writing. So we might judge society to have been partially "journalized" somewhere between the 1880s and the 1920s, at least in North America and many parts of Europe, as well as Australia, Japan, and elsewhere. Journalization would advance much more with radio news, with newsreels shown in movie houses, with television news, and then with a deluge of TV news with the advent of cable TV news and, ever so much more, with the accelerating pace of news in the digital era that we access not only from newspapers, magazines, radio, and television, but from desktop computers in offices, personal computers at home, laptops we can carry with us, and smartphones that seem a veritable part of the human body for hundreds of millions of people.

Drama, in 1974, Williams insisted, had by no means been superseded but it was also by no means "coextensive with theatre." Today, journalism has by no means been superseded, but it is no longer coextensive with what fits upon an oversized page or within the 20 or 30 minutes of a television news broadcast. And it seems to me that honest journalists must come to a conclusion much like Williams's – that the texts, conventions, and practices that they had long taken to be obviously the core of their field were suddenly problematic because "these others are there." Today, many journalistic others are there. There is no ignoring the efforts of citizen journalists whose cellphone cameras provide the first authoritative news of street protests in Cairo or terror bombings in London or police shootings in the United States. There is no ignoring the online news outfits that – often operated by a handful of people or even a single person from kitchen table or bedroom – break important news stories. Josh Marshall's TalkingPointsMemo, launched as a blog in 2000, was the first poster child for this work. but there are many others, too, from Tehran Bureau covering news of Iran from London to NK News similarly covering North Korea from London and other online sites that Soomin Seo has dubbed "virtual foreign bureaus."[7] Many others cover local or regional news. Among the first of these was Voice of San Diego (voiceofsandiego. org) established in 2005, MinnPost (minnpost.com) in 2007, and Texas Tribune (texastribune.org) in 2009, all of them still in operation. Still others are increasingly important in covering specific topics, like Inside Climate News (2007), in 2013 the first of the small start-ups to win a Pulitzer Prize; and the Marshall Project (2014), which won a Pulitzer Prize in 2016 for work jointly undertaken with ProPublica (2007), itself a celebrated and much larger news nonprofit already with two Pulitzer Prizes to its name. There is no failing to note that the premier crowd-sourced phenomenon of the past decade, Wikipedia, has become an indispensable news source, its entries updated almost instantaneously when a noted individual either arrives at a birthday or dies, a significant election takes place, and so on. Nor are people speechless if you ask them what blog or website they go to regularly for news of their field – the mortgage business, constitutional law, developments of interest and importance in sociology, and so forth, and this in a world in which journalists initially took blogging to be a laughable, if not an enemy, enterprise.

It was as recently as 2005 that Svennik Hoyer and Horst Pottker wrote about the establishment, first in the United States, of "the news paradigm" that during the past century spread to Europe and has been accepted as the leading model of how professional journalists should report the news.[8] That paradigm consists of the central use of interviewing as a news-gathering technique, the use of an inverted pyramid presentational structure in news stories, and the premise of "objectivity" as the reporter's moral and literary stance.[9] The acceptance of this model in European journalism was slow and uneven: "Gradual developments over several decades seem to be the normal conditions in news journalism," Hoyer and John Nonseid concluded in their chapter on Norway.[10] Slow, uneven, but in the end powerful, even as some European countries confine its influence more than others.[11]

Hoyer and Nonseid report on a Swedish study by Inger Lindstedt in which she examines Swedish news textbooks from 1917 to 1996 and finds the texts rejecting this news paradigm before World War II. They referred to the inverted pyramid presentation of news as "American" as late as 1953. By 1981 it was called either "international" or even, by then, "traditional." In less than 30 years, "American" had become "traditional" and "the news paradigm" had taken on the air of inevitability that "traditional" signifies.[12] But the journalization of society, the journalization of human experience, was not inevitable. It was a complex social transformation, as chapter 3 has indicated, and one that happened at a different pace and in different forms in different nations.

The American press in the late nineteenth century, the British press early in the twentieth century, and the Dutch press only after 1945 came to offer readers an edited, planned, visual mapping of news displayed across the newspaper page and laid out also within each story. In each case, journalists asserted growing control in telling readers what the most important information is and, as Marcel Broersma memorably put it, coming to accept that they should no longer be expected "merely to record happenings but to extract the news from an event."[13]

The recency of recognizably contemporary journalism can be seen also in Britain, where there was nothing that *read* like modern journalism until about 1920. This is the persuasive argument of Donald Matheson's study of British news discourse – as he puts it, the birth of news discourse in Britain, between 1880 and 1930. It is not, in his view, that there was no such thing as news in newspapers in 1880. There were newspapers. There were even reporters. But the model of what a newspaper did in 1880 was that it served as "a collection of raw information" and what it typically had become by 1930 was "a form of knowledge in itself, not dependent on other discourses to be able to make statements about the world."[14] The Victorian newspaper was "a medley of various public styles, voices and types of text" in the late nineteenth century. It is not until around 1920 that one can recognize that "a journalistic discourse has emerged, which allows the news to subsume these various voices under a universal, standard voice."[15]

These studies of the visuality of the front page (Broersma on the Netherlands) and the verbal discourse of the front page (Matheson on Britain) both locate the emergence of today's leading forms of contemporary journalism in the twentieth century and not before. And this is not, it seems to me, just a matter of changing fashion in artistic or literary presentation. We can see vast changes in formal style in, say, the novel over the past several centuries, but one has little doubt that Charles Dickens in the 1850s and F. Scott Fitzgerald in the 1920s and Toni Morrison in our own time, or Jane Austen in the early 1800s and Virginia Woolf in the early 1900s and Margaret Atwood today could all plausibly, in one's imagination, sit together on the same television talk show to discuss "the novel." They would understand one another as engaged in essentially the same project. This seems much less likely – basically impossible – with journalists of 1820 and 1850 and journalists of 1920 and 1950 and today. The journalism that we know – despite its many variations and the sometimes radical changes it is undergoing today online – understands that it is offering some sort of knowledge about contemporary public events, however vaguely defined the character of this knowledge may be, and this is a much more serious, ambitious, and self-conscious belief than eighteenth- or nineteenth-century news-writers conceived for themselves. They were relaying information from hither and yon, took little or no responsibility for its validity, and threw into the mix a miscellany of items, often written by others, whose greatest redeeming value was that it filled empty space on the page.

Somewhere between roughly 1920 and roughly 1950 the voice of contemporary journalism took hold. The Americans got there a touch earlier, with the technique of interviewing giving shape to US journalism by the 1880s and 1890s, and the summary lead and inverted pyramid form offering a common vantage for asserting the authority of journalistic discourse by around 1910. But nineteenth-century American journalism until the last two decades of the nineteenth century was frequently quite a lot like the "Victorian" journalism that Matheson describes as dominating the entire Victorian era in Britain.

When Daniel Hallin adapted the phrase "high modernism" to name the period of American journalism ascendant from World War II to the early years of the Vietnam War, what caught his eye, in an interview with war correspondent Peter Arnett, was Arnett's unbending allegiance to objective reporting, and "the absence of a sense of doubt or contradiction."[16]

That self-assurance has never entirely disappeared. Professionalism as a set of values is still more often sworn by than sworn at in leading news organizations, and certainly in the halls of journalism schools.[17] Journalism at the national level became substantially more critical from the 1970s on and while there are ebbs and flows of complacency still, the journalistic insouciance of the 1950s is irretrievable. (The American case is not by any means unique, as a striking historical study of Swedish public broadcasting indicates.)[18]

All this suggests that the recent radical changes in journalism – resulting from the new technologies of satellite, cable television, online news forms, converged multimedia newsrooms, and the vast upheavals in "business models" that have sustained most influential news organizations for most of the past century – do not represent a shift from a settled brand of journalism. At any rate, if journalism was settled, it was a settled practice, as the Swedish textbooks suggest, that came to be thought of as "traditional" even though it was established within living memory, and borrowed from American and British models.

If societies became journalized from roughly 1890 to 1970, there is nonetheless something new afoot today, something that is clearly related to the internet but not reducible to it, something that I want to suggest is far more about how news reaches audiences and settles into their lives than it is about how journalists produce the "content" audiences depend upon. The change is one in culture and meaning, it resides in the symbolic interstices that guide how people spend their time, how they imagine possibilities for themselves or their children, how they adjust and readjust their horizons. And I don't know a better guide to sketching in what has been happening in the past several decades than to revisit Williams's five propositions to see where they do or do not illuminate the transformation of journalism, and of ourselves as inhabitants of a journalized world.

Williams's Five Propositions Adapted to a Journalized Society

The variety of journalistic forms

The digital revolution has inspired a rapidly multiplying variety of journalisms. Radio brought the news bulletin, film brought the newsreel and later the documentary, television gave us the news briefs that have dominated television news for most of its life, opening up into a greater variety of formats with the news magazine (notably, in the US, with "60 Minutes" in 1968) and later, with 24-hour cable news, personalized news shows organized around a single opinionated entertainer. But the digital opened the world in a far greater variety of ways, blending and streaming media with abandon.

The blog may be the fountainhead of online innovation. There were digital magazines early on – *Slate* and *Salon* – but these lively publications were indeed online magazines, reproducing on screens rather than on paper a variety of opinion, advocacy, and review, just what you might find in a classy print-era magazine of public affairs, culture, and the arts.

The blog was different. It was, as its origins in the word "weblog" indicates, a log or diary. But it was backwards. The most recent entry appeared at the beginning, not at the end. It made the diary or journal news. And it could be about any topic under the sun – or a grab-bag of topics. It could be shared with a few or made available to anyone interested. And it could be as inward-looking as a private journal, as in the plethora of "mommy blogs," or it could be devoutly outward-looking, like the legal blogs Lawfare and SCOTUS-blog (SCOTUS stands for "Supreme Court of the United States") and The Volokh Conspiracy.

Our new media are digital, yes. They are also, we might say, megaphonic. They amplify the Power of One. But there are, for instance, "Mommy forums" as well as "Mommy blogs," and many other discussion groups and bulletin boards that welcome conversational back-and-forth on an endless assortment of special interest topics.

Journalism in the rhythms of everyday life

Journalism organized in the form of newspapers began to be a part of everyday life for some people early on. By the 1930s, the American humorist Will Rogers wrote of how essential the newspaper was to his breakfast. "Take away my bacon, take away my eggs if you must, but I cannot have a breakfast without my newspaper!" People consumed news at specific times of day – the newspaper at the breakfast table, the evening television news (in the US) over dinner or just before or just after dinner. And in one of the most clever studies of the news ever conducted, Bernard Berelson and colleagues interviewed New Yorkers during a long newspaper strike in their city in 1945, asking them what (if anything) they missed about the newspaper that was suddenly unavailable to them. The result surprised the researchers: it was not the newspaper as instrument of gathering intelligence about one topic or another that they missed most. In fact, although nearly everyone they interviewed affirmed the view that newspapers are valuable in transmitting serious information to citizens, only one in three could pick from a list of six continuing stories one that they "missed" being able to follow during the strike (and remember that this was the summer of 1945 – World War II was ongoing in the Asian theater). One of the features people missed most was news as "a tool for daily living," notably following favorite radio programs "without the radio log published in the newspaper."

Perhaps most striking of all is that people missed "reading itself regardless of content." They found reading "a strongly and pleasurably motivated act." If they did not have a newspaper to read, the next best thing was "whatever came to hand" – books or old magazines lying around the house. What mattered was the having-something-to-read in particular moments of the day. Journalism had become a habit and one to which they felt a genuine attachment. But it was the habit, not the news, that mattered most. Berelson found this a "ritualistic and near-compulsive" feature of their lives, especially the use of the newspaper as a secondary activity while people did something else – eating or traveling to work.[19]

Journalism also provided organized breaks from habit. At a time (1930s–1950s) when newspapers might produce "extra" editions if there was a very important breaking news story, this was a special moment and a signal that something of significance had happened. And television likewise could produce what would later be called "media events" in covering some news-out-of-its-dailiness event live on camera, whether it be the Kennedy assassination or the Kennedy funeral or Anwar Sadat's visit to Jerusalem or the royal wedding of Diana and Charles.[20] This would be marked by the newsreader's hushed and reverential tone, likely the absence of commercial interruptions in news systems where the commercial break was routine.

Journalism has done all this and more. But, again, the digital transformation of journalism has integrated news into life in novel and powerful ways. Strangely enough, Raymond Williams offered us the best term for this transformation, although he did not live to see smartphones: "mobile privatization." During a year spent at Stanford University in 1972–73, where he wrote his short book *Television: Technology and Cultural Form*, he coined this term to refer to "the particularity of the newly social, one might say suburban world with which radio and television were to engage," as Roger Silverstone would observe in a 2003 edition of the book. This was, Silverstone writes, a world of "increasing individualization and fragmentation."[21] It is hard to think of a term that does more to describe, or at least to begin to describe, what mobile phones have done to people's posture, to their concentrated focus on the object held in their hands as they walk down the street, sit on the bus or subway, or, heaven help them and us, as they drive their cars. In 2009, I was interviewing two *Wall Street Journal* reporters at a restaurant on their lunch hour, and realized at one point that both were looking directly at their phones while I was trying in vain to address them – not only that, there was nothing in their demeanor to suggest that they felt they were being at all rude. It would be some years before I would do something similar – and to my wife, no less! I apologized, but still: if that is not mobile privatization, I don't know what is.

And yet, this is a most complicated matter. People stay in touch with one another at great distances, even if they separate themselves from people physically present. These behaviors have become part of us. People's telephones were part of their homes; now they are nearly a part of their bodies.

The dissolving separation of professionals and spectators

Here, too, what Williams says about drama makes sense for journalism. As media scholar and director of the University of Iowa journalism program David Ryfe put it, "the boundaries of journalism are blurring. It is increasingly difficult to distinguish the inside from the outside of the field."[22] Still, on this point, for drama Williams was only half right. In many respects, for all of the experimental theater and improvisational comedy, and taking of theater to the street, and having actors stationed in the audience or bringing members of the audience on stage, and much more, with the perspective of more than 40 years of further development in theater, the division between actors and audience has shown great endurance. Here and there it has adopted some informality from the experiments of the 1960s, but enclosed them within the disciplined divide between professionals on stage and audiences in their seats. Only in rare instances did the blurring of the actor/audience divide prove ultimately successful. In the 1990s BBC serial drama *House of Cards*, the lead character, politician Francis Urquhart, frequently stepped out of the action to briefly address the television audience directly, and in the 2013 American adaptation on Netflix, actor Kevin Spacey's Francis Underwood character does the same. But this theatrical gesture, that Shakespeare also employed, is more of a wry reminder of the separation between action on stage and the recognition that a theater piece is a fiction and theater-going is the reality that sustains it – it reinforces more than it undercuts the actor–audience divide. (Netflix has plans for its *Adventures of Puss in Boots* series for children to become interactive, with the viewer having an opportunity to choose one of several plot directions at different points in the story. A Netflix spokesperson, Carla Engelbrecht, said that viewers should hold on to the remote and not lose it in the couch cushions: "We need you to lean forward a little bit to engage with the choices."[23] My prediction, based on the theatrical past, is that this Netflix innovation will go exactly nowhere.)

What is the case with journalism? Despite the impressive contributions to journalism from complete amateurs who happen to be in the right place at the right time to broadcast news from their cellphone or cellphone camera before professional journalists get to the scene, this influences one relatively small portion of the journalistic scene – the journalist (or amateur journalist or citizen journalist) as eyewitness.

There is more of this citizen eyewitnessing than there used to be, although we should not exaggerate the difference from the past. News has frequently originated in "tips" that amateurs handed reporters, free of charge. What's new is that the amateurs can publish their "news tips" directly on their own blogs or on their Facebook page or their Twitter account. They can bypass the "gatekeeper" journalists they once would have been dependent upon. Still, almost all news transmitted by mainstream news organizations – print, digital, television, and radio – still originates in the work of professional journalists at legacy news organizations, a talented troupe of full-time freelancers, and a small group of journalists at online-only digital-native organizations. Most stories that matter require research, context, interviews, and a feel for what makes a story. Citizen journalists make a contribution, certainly, but most often when they happen upon events that are themselves self-evidently stories – a bomb explodes, a fire burns a forest or a home – things that practically say out loud, "Report me! Record me!" The expert reporter, in contrast, can see news behind a façade of normalcy or eventlessness. A citizen journalist needs to happen upon an event that all but writes its own headline.

The growing problem of representing a complex, global, integrated society

Williams held that we depend more than ever on representations, including dramatic representations, because societies have become so very difficult to represent. That is to say that societies achieve something by representing society to itself. Most of us spend most of our time living life without knowing quite what we are doing. It is useful to us to have life summarized, highlighted, narrated, dramatized in ways that help us make sense of what we ourselves experience.

Years ago I watched my nephew, then just two or three, fall down in the living-room, various members of his family sitting around him. He looked toward his mother and father as if he were pondering the following question: How bad was that fall? Was it bad enough for me to cry? His lip curled toward tears but, seeing no notable alarm from Mom or Dad, he decided the answer to his question must be "no" and he did not cry.

But when does complexity become unmanageable in the way that Williams suggests it has become? To a scientist, a poet, or an artist, the world has been amazingly complex for centuries. When you think about something as unchanging but as central as pregnancy and childbirth, the complex coordination a growing fetus in the womb engineers with the mother is simply astonishing – or rather, unsimple but astonishing. Pregnancy has been complex from its distant evolutionary beginnings, and it is no more nor less complex today. But a growing sense of complexity or consciousness of complexity – yes, that seems to be our fate, even with pregnancy.

Walter Lippmann pointed out in 1922 how difficult it was for people to comprehend the world when so much of it came to them – necessarily – through representations and not direct experience. And in the 1920s and 1930s journalists increasingly complained that their jobs had become intensely more difficult exactly because the world around them was growing so much more complex. We may look back nearly a century later and wonder what they were complaining about! People still lived as much in rural towns and villages as in cities; they rarely traveled more than 50 miles from the homes they grew up in, they died from the same set of diseases – mostly communicable diseases and not degenerative ones – that people had been dying from for ages. The US remained largely isolated from the rest of the world – and ignorant of it. Still, journalists in the 1920s and 1930s began to recognize that facts did not speak for themselves, that facts laid out without interpretation were insufficient in a world where local affairs were growing more integrated with policy made in Washington, and Washington policy itself was more responsive to an international system of states and markets that the United States was increasingly enmeshed in.[24]

All that acknowledged, the world has indeed grown still more incomprehensible. For one thing, at least in Europe and North America, though this is less true of other parts of the world, "God's will" as an explanation of incomprehensible developments has proved less and less satisfying. It may provide some solace – but solace is not comprehension. And we have powerful instances of radically incomprehensible events and changes. The moral incomprehensibility of the Holocaust (and a succession of genocides) makes one wonder what there is about human beings that we can still be proud of.

The grounding of journalistic representation in the context of the local, the bodily, and the familial

We are enveloped by and engaged with and enchanted with our various new digitally empowered means – but we employ them most of all for entirely familiar ends. The most popular websites and apps support people's exploration of health and illness; dating and sexuality and porn; advice and support on fertility and pregnancy and nursing and motherhood, on travel and transportation across large distances beyond one's own home or small distances (by Uber or Lyft) within a few miles of home; renting an apartment, buying a house, finding a job, choosing a car or movie or vacuum cleaner, a pre-school or a college. These are almost all ordinary experiences we managed without digital media, without Amazon or Netflix or Uber or Airbnb. We use digital media to buy and sell, the same way – only more efficiently – that we used classified advertising in newspapers not so long ago.

In some ways, it is clear that we pursue our old objectives in substantially new or different ways. People still meet and make romantic attachments in school classrooms, in bars, in chance encounters, in church social groups. But we also meet online, sometimes learning much less – but sometimes much more – about the person than in settings where face-to-face meetings came first.

Journalism, in its beginnings, had little to do with the local. Early newspapers transmitted almost exclusively foreign news. Newspapers began to connect to everyday life only in the nineteenth century by advertising consumer goods and by giving more attention to coverage of political and economic affairs within a locality and, over time, of society and sport and fashion, as well as crime and legal proceedings.

Nothing here is meant to suggest that journalism since the early 2000s is going through the exact same cultural revolution that Raymond Williams saw taking place in drama in the 1960s. Nowhere in what Williams wrote is there reference to "networks" of association and communication; nowhere in his 1974 inaugural lecture is there reference to some of the key terms that characterize the world of news today – notably, "search" (which, wrote sociologist David Stark, "is the watchword of the information age.");[25] or "sharing" (about which Nicholas John has written the thoughtful and prescient *The Age of Sharing*).[26] But what can we learn, nonetheless, from the similarities?

We can learn or re-learn not to lift technology out of the societies where it exists or out of the daily lives in which it gets embedded. Nor for that matter should we isolate it from the aspirations that shaped the technologies in the first place, as Fred Turner has perhaps shown best in documenting the ways that the intentions and aspirations of the emerging world of Silicon Valley were rooted in the counter-culture of the 1960s.[27] We can learn that social context matters. Perhaps most of all, we can ponder the point Williams makes that there is a need that grows more urgent, not less, for comprehensible representations of the world around us, a world that has grown ever more global in the past half-century, ever more characterized by people moving across it through trade or tourism, or through displacement by wars, famines, and natural disasters, or through the strong force of a fervent hope that they could have better lives in some other location. When people's construction of meaning for their lives cannot even take for granted the persistence of the home and place where they were born, the search for representations and images of what life is and what it can be become ever more important. As Williams argued, we need dramas, representations, fictions – and, with journalism, true stories to represent us to ourselves, and we need them more than ever.

7

The Crisis in News: Can You Whistle a Happy Tune?

This chapter was prepared for an international conference in Barcelona in May 2014 and substantially revised for the 2016 publication of conference papers in Jeffrey C. Alexander, Elizabeth Butler Breese, and Maria Luengo, eds., *The Crisis of Journalism Reconsidered* (Cambridge University Press).

The first newspaper in the world was published in Strasbourg in 1605, if we mean by "newspaper" a vehicle for organized news-gathering published on paper in a recurrent, periodical form for a general audience.[1] The newspaper, then, first appeared in what historians of Europe call the "early modern" era. Like other elements of modernity that date to the 1600s and early 1700s – like the controlled experiment or the novel – it is a cultural form that we have come to take for granted as constitutive of our world. The controlled experiment remains a vital part of liberal societies to this day. Even the novel, whose death has been regularly announced for generations, continues its spirited life.[2]

And newspapers? For some years now, it has been strongly argued that we are in the endgame of the distribution of news on paper.[3] The argument was renewed in 2014 by the late David Carr, the savvy media reporter for the *New York Times*, who died unexpectedly in February 2015. Carr noted that in the space of a week in August 2014, three major US news companies – Gannett, Tribune Company, and E. W. Scripps – spun off their newspaper properties from their multimedia empires. The flurry of divestitures, he wrote, looked like "one of those movies about global warming where icebergs calve huge chunks into churning waters."[4] Carr reported discouraging numbers, but even more alarming were his metaphors. He compared divesting the newspaper properties after a decade of stripping them of their resources to "trashing a house by burning all the furniture to stay warm and then inviting people in to see if they want to buy the joint." And while he blamed "the natural order" of the marketplace, he found no solace or hope in the public. Many people, he wrote, "haven't cared or noticed as their hometown newspapers have reduced staffing, days of circulation, delivery and coverage." Are they likely to notice or care "when those newspapers go away altogether? I'm not optimistic about that."[5]

This is the same man who stood up at the podium of a 2009 journalism conference to make some remarks, then returned to the speakers' table to pick up his laptop and, holding it up above his head as he returned to the podium, declared: "I have more resources for reporting in my hand at this moment than in any newsroom I have ever worked in."[6] It was a simple, dramatic gesture and he was of course absolutely right. He was right for reporters and editors. He was right, too, for news consumers who also have laptops (and now smart phones) and can access the websites of hundreds, thousands of news organizations around the world. It is, with all the irony the term suggests, a brave new world for information. How did we get here – and so fast! And what should we feel about it? The despair of Carr 2014? Or the awestruck wonder of Carr 2009? Or are we doomed, until the day the last newspaper lands outside the door of our house or apartment, to yo-yo up and down from wonder to despair and back again, victims of a civic bipolar disorder?

A week after Carr's 2014 column, one of the most consistently perceptive observers of the news scene, Clay Shirky, published a piece (online), "Last Call: The End of the Printed Newspaper." Shirky warned, "If you are a journalist at a print publication, your job is in danger. Period. Time to do something about it." It is too late, he advised, to say that the future of print "remains unclear." Shirky says:

The future of print remains what? Try to imagine a world where the future of print is unclear: Maybe 25-year-olds will start demanding news from yesterday, delivered in an unshareable format once a day. Perhaps advertisers will decide "Click to buy" is for wimps. Mobile phones: could be a fad. After all, anything could happen with print. Hard to tell, really.[7]

Of American 25–34-year-olds surveyed in 2000, 41 percent reported reading a newspaper "yesterday"; in 2013 it was 21 percent. Of college graduates in 2000, 61 percent read a newspaper yesterday; in 2013, it was 37 percent.[8] It's a downhill slide and the hill is steep.

I do not dispute what Carr or Shirky have said; even so, their conclusions are incomplete. I do not reject their views, but I do want to redraw them. I will try to do so here by identifying several factors that make the profound change they point to – and I agree that it is profound – something less of a force of nature than they represent it, something less of the decisive break in the history of newspapers, and something less than catastrophe for civic knowledge. For me, the conclusion is something less than optimism but a watchfulness on a scene where there remain grounds for hope.

A Broader Context for the Decline of the Printed Newspaper

Printed newspapers will in time, possibly a very short time, largely disappear. But while the shrinking of the professional journalistic workforce has already disrupted tens of thousands of lives, its impact on the quality of civic life and political knowledge is far from settled. Several points are essential to any general evaluation.

First, the phenomena that Carr and Shirky accurately depict are most intense in the United States, even though the digital transformation that launched them is global. What accounts for this, as many have noted, is that the economic fuel of American print journalism has throughout the twentieth century been much more predominantly based on advertising than is the case for print journalism in European and other liberal democracies. European newspapers have been more dependent on subscriptions and daily purchase, have been less lavish with pages and space, and consequently their shrinkage has not so far been catastrophic.[9] The economic crisis of journalism in Europe has been more gradual.

Europe has also been steadied by the rock of public broadcasting and a greater willingness of many European states to intervene with direct financial support for newspapers, too. Still, European newspapers also face a declining demand for their print editions with the relentless demographic fact that older people read print-on-paper far more than people in their 30s and 40s who read print newspapers more than people in their teens and 20s. As laptops become more portable and popular and as smart phones become more versatile, multifaceted, and omnipresent, the tumble downhill will continue. The pace of the descent, however, is accelerated in the United States thanks to prevailing forces both economic (the dependence on advertising) and political (the resistance to government interventions). In different political and economic settings, the impact of digital communications on journalism differs.

Second, print newspaper organizations as such disappeared 10–20 years ago. Where do you find a print-only news organization? If that is what we are talking about, the headstone can already be chiseled: The Print Newspaper, 1605–2000. The second date acknowledges the importance of the World Wide Web as the medium for e-commerce that all but eliminated classified advertising in newspapers: eBay launched in 1995; the employment website, monster.com, went public at the end of 1996; and Craigslist became a for-profit company in 1999. The question since 1999 has only been whether newspaper-spawned websites can attract enough advertising to subsidize their print editions. There is no reason at this point to believe this will be so. That does not mean, however, that newspaper-based organizations cannot place their websites behind pay walls in a way that pulls news organizations as a whole into economic viability. The following newspapers already have more than 100,000 paid digital subscribers: the *New York Times*, the *New York Post*, the *New York Daily News*, *Newsday*, the *Newark Star-Ledger*, the *Los Angeles Times*, and the *Denver Post*. They may still sell print editions, at premium prices, for several decades to serve people addicted to newsprint with their morning coffee or on their morning commute. Few in this print market will be around in 40 years, or even 30, but news organizations may still find pricing that works if distribution costs can be contained – by limiting home delivery to the city and the nearest suburbs only; by ending home delivery; by printing only a few days a week rather than seven or printing only on Sundays. There are 25 newspapers around the country that by online or print reach half or more of adults in their metropolitan area on an average day – from Rochester, New York to Honolulu, Hawaii, Richmond, Virginia to El Paso, Texas, and Columbus, Ohio to San Diego, California. That should make them uniquely valuable for both civic health and advertising advantage. Overall, combined print and paid online circulation of American dailies has held steady from 1992 to 2012 – actually, it has shown some slight increase, a fact that has received scant attention.[10]

All this is to say that there are no "newspapers" any more as stand-alone enterprises; all newspapers are part of newspaper-and-online businesses. We do not know how much the professional expertise of the print side powers the technological advances of the online side, either in an individual journalist or in the collective enterprise. Many of the most popular websites, and most of those that are most widely respected, are of traditional print or broadcast news organizations. Those organizations are changing, and scrambling, but few of them are disappearing.

Third, there remains a market for "long-form" printed journalism, very long form. Consider the number of books by American journalists about the wars in Iraq and Afghanistan. Remember, Americans are notoriously bored by foreign affairs – although less so by wars that involve Americans. Still, we now have books on American wars in Iraq and Afghanistan by NBC correspondent Richard Engel (*War Journal*, 2008), National Public Radio reporter Anne Garrels (*Naked in Baghdad*, 2003), *US News* military correspondent Linda Robinson (*Tell Me How This Ends*, 2008), *Wall Street Journal* Baghdad correspondent Farnaz Fassihi (*Waiting for an Ordinary Day*, 2008), *New York Times* military reporter Michael R. Gordon (*Cobra II*, 2006), the late *Washington Post* reporter Anthony Shadid (*Night Draws Near*, 2006; *House of Stone*, 2012), *Washington Post* reporter Rajiv Chandrasekaran (*Imperial Life in the Emerald City*, 2006; *Little America*, 2012), several books by *Washington Post* editor Bob Woodward (*Plan of Attack*, 2004; *State of Denial*, 2006; *The War Within*, 2008; *Obama's Wars*, 2010), *Washington Post* reporter David Finkel (*The Good Soldiers*, 2009;*Thank You For Your Service*, 2013), *Newsweek* reporter Michael Isikoff (*Hubris*, 2006), *Washington Post* reporter Thomas Ricks (*Fiasco*, 2006; *Gamble*, 2009) *New Yorker* reporter George Packer (*The Assassins' Gate*, 2006; *Betrayed*, 2008), *Washington Post* reporter Steve Coll (*Ghost Wars*, 2005; *The Bin Ladens*, 2008) *Wall Street Journal* reporter Ron Suskind (*The One Percent Doctrine*, 2006) – and more. What do their publishers think they are doing? It is one thing to publish Bob Woodward, whose books are all but guaranteed to be bestsellers. But the other dozen listed here, although well known among their fellow journalists, are not exactly household names.

Who reads this stuff? Enough people to make it a reasonable venture. For a publisher, it is a small and ordinary risk to pay one reporter an advance on royalties; it is not like maintaining a newsroom of 500 or 1,000 professionals, nor even like supporting a Baghdad bureau of five. In effect, the struggling news organizations that employ these various reporters in a small way support the rattled but still profitable publishing business by training and employing expert journalists who turn to book-writing with real authority. The larger point is that the rapid-fire circulation of cute cat videos has not replaced long-form journalism. There is more book-length journalism than ever. The shrinking of the newsroom is larger than the shrinking of serious journalism. Is serious journalism in fact shrinking?

Fourth, in the United States, as in Europe and most other parts of the world, most people get their news from television. In the Pew Research Center's biennial survey of popular attitudes toward the media, conducted in July, 2013, 69 percent of people listed television as their "main" source of news (they could list up to two "mains"), 50 percent digital sources, and 28 percent newspapers.[11] Television is easy and convenient, and that is not a bad thing. It communicates the basics, sometimes vividly, which is about as much as most of us can absorb most of the time. With larger and larger, better and better TV screens, it beats the pants off of what you can see on a mobile phone. What follows from this is that the plight of the newspaper is not something that a very large proportion of Americans experience as opening up some notable gap – or any gap – in their lives. More Americans have reported television as their primary source of news rather than newspapers for about 50 years. Most people do not understand or do not care that television gets *its* news from newspapers. At the nation's 50 state capitals, newspapers plus wire services field 410 full-time reporters, television 88. And 86 percent of local television stations do not have a single reporter, full time or part time, at the state capital.[12]

Fifth, if what really matters for the social and civic welfare is not the disappearance of a paper product tossed on the doorstep but the thinning of fair-minded, analytical, and watchdog news reporting, how much of a decline – if any – are we witnessing? If such news can be provided by some means other than newspapers and by some organizations or mechanisms able to pay for the Baghdad bureau and to pay lawyers when libel suits arise, the civic value of journalism can be sustained.

There are more than 1,350 daily printed newspapers in the United States, even though essentially all of them are part of businesses that also publish online. Few of them have ever won a Pulitzer Prize or opened a foreign bureau or supported a full-time foreign correspondent or, for that matter, a full-time or part-time correspondent in its own state capital. It could, of course, be worse – and it was. H. L. Mencken, that notoriously acerbic soul, who recalled that when he began in journalism in the 1890s most cities were dominated by "dreadful little rags, venal, vulnerable, and vile." The newspapers I read growing up in the 1950s and 1960s were far better; they were merely insipid, incurious, and inbred. There is research to back up that ungenerous judgment. One useful study by Carl Sessions Stepp, long a columnist for *American Journalism Review*, compared a dozen major regional metro dailies for 1964 and 1999 and concluded – I cannot imagine any other conclusion possible – that the 1999 papers were "by almost any measure, far superior to their 1960s counterparts: better written, better looking, better organized, more responsible, less sensational, less sexist and racist, and more informative and public-spirited than they are often given credit for."[13]

All this suggests to me that despair about the future of news should be put in perspective. Granted, newspapers plus the Associated Press have been, and in 2014 remain, the backbone of US news-gathering. Probably the most agile and influential new contributor to original reporting in the past half century is public radio, although its contribution to local reporting is in most of its outlets very slight. Collectively, the online nonprofits are impressive and some of them may prove to have staying power. But the newspaper-based news organizations remain, their newsroom populations and budgets slashed, the giants.

It is worth being nostalgic for newspapers that not only relayed interesting and sometimes useful information to members of a geographic community, but that spoke for and represented those communities to themselves. Even so, few of these news organizations ever showed much acumen for "watchdog" journalism. Not many made a great investment in local news-gathering. Not many provided much analytical depth apart from a few syndicated columnists. Most of the news they printed was handed to them – sometimes literally. This was especially so in business reporting, which barely merited the term "reporting." In 2002, journalist Robert Samuelson remembered joining the business staff at the *Washington Post* in 1969 – one of seven staffers in the department (there had been only one business writer when Ben Bradlee became the paper's editor in 1965; by 2002, there would be a staff of 85). In 1969 the business "page" (no section) was "tucked behind the sports section." At that time, "[c]ritical reporting was often conspicuous by its absence. Business reporters were far down the status ladder. They were often viewed as being not much better than corporate flacks."[14]

Moreover, the 1960s and 1970s brought for the first time in the history of US journalism a recognition that the narrow demography of the newsroom contributed to a narrow focus in news coverage – there were hardly any minority employees and the few women employees were largely confined to writing on fashion and high society. That, too, changed in the 1970s – not enough perhaps, but enough to make a big difference. American journalism after 1968 became more diverse, more critical, more investigative, more thoughtful than ever before.

Newspapers were theoretically a pillar of democratic self-government, but in practice their publishers were interested in a good return on their investment, not in fostering democracy. I think the US journalistic world from about 1968 to about 2005 was something to be proud of, despite its shortcomings. This was a relatively brief period, not part of an unbroken tradition of great reporting. It was brief but deep in cementing among thousands of journalists an ambitious and public-minded sense of mission. That sense of a strong civic obligation and opportunity became more central than ever before to how reporters understood their jobs – not only at the 50–100 best newspapers, but also at the next 1,300, even though the latter group provided relatively little local institutional support for their idealistic employees.

What is so profoundly different today is not a change from a settled, static set of practices flash-frozen in 1791 with the First Amendment, or in the 1920s when Walter Lippmann bemoaned the limited ability of journalism to serve its democratic aspirations, or at any other single point. Changes were already under way inside and outside journalism, particularly in the 1970s well before the digital revolution shook the news business to its core.

Democracies after 1945, and even more fully from the 1960s on, including in the United States, became "monitory democracies" or "counter-democracies" (in the language of John Keane and Pierre Rosanvallon respectively).[15] Specifically, this means that they rely less on elections organized by parties and more on holding elected officials accountable through a broad set of mechanisms: a more aggressive and critical press; a growing involvement of citizens in social movements and other forms of active political protest; the proliferation of organized public interest groups; and the institutionalization of accountability requirements, inspections, investigations, and transparency practices inside government itself. Journalism's role in monitory democracies grew as news professionals self-consciously took on the "watchdog" role in holding governments accountable and an interpretive role in helping audiences make sense of the complex and distant events in national capitals and around the globe that touched citizens' everyday lives.

What people hope for from the best journalism is not all played out. It will have new recruits, it will find an audience, and it will contribute usefully to self-government. Let me turn more closely to how news production is changing. I think there are grounds here for at least a cautious optimism. Full-bodied optimism about anything in human affairs is incautious and no doubt we should be grateful for leadership from those imbued with it, but in my armchair, my expectations for the news business are more measured.

News Production in Transition

Goldfish bowl

Reporters covering news, especially those covering events or activities that attract a great deal of attention, are monitored in the very course of their work by a variety of others as never before. In the "old days" – the 1970s and 1980s – reporters on a presidential campaign trail, for example, could joke around with one another, could have moments of privacy or collegial confidentiality as they went about their business. This is much less true today. "People are watching you," said one CBS News reporter who covered Hillary Clinton's 2008 campaign. "Now that everybody has a Flip cam, they're looking to get you." The late Helen Thomas, for 57 years a correspondent for the news agency UPI and, in 2010, just shy of her 90th birthday and working for Hearst Newspapers, criticized Israel in a brief interview with a little known Jewish affairs website. Thomas judged Israel to be an aggressor against Palestinians and recommended that Jews in Israel return to where they had come from in Poland and Germany as well as the United States. People who had worked closely with her quickly dissociated themselves, invitations were withdrawn, awards named after her renamed.[16]

The mutual surveillance is not primarily face-to-face, but online. There is less opportunity for editors to lavish time and attention on reporters' work, but a hundred thousand editors have bloomed online, ready to suggest, correct, critique, or attack for sins factual, grammatical, political, ideological, and imaginary.

Clicks

Online "metrics" for measuring how frequently readers "click" on particular news items (and sometimes how long they stay there) are available from commercial firms to news organizations and, essentially, all news organizations of any size purchase such services and use these click counts to measure the popularity of individual pieces. They thereby learn what kind of stories are popular, what kind of stories are likely to draw in more readers and improve the attractiveness of the news organization's website and the cash value of particular reporters. Before the digital era, evaluations of this sort were far more difficult to undertake, even though by informal means ("buzz") some reporters could become very well known as unusually appealing to large audiences. Now, however, this is everyday practice, it is widespread throughout news businesses.

Even so, editors at some news organizations prefer to keep the knowledge of "click" success to themselves rather than parading it before the newsroom to shower implicit praise or implicit blame upon individuals. They want journalists to be judged by journalistic criteria more than by marketplace success – and they, the editors, want to maintain control in the news-making process.[17] That said, awareness of marketplace success appears to be more salient in the lives of working journalists than ever before. Some news sites have chosen to pay writers by the click. The celebrity-focused news site Gawker (which closed in 2016) paid new recruits during a 90-day trial period $1,500 a month – with bonuses up to $6,000 pegged to the numbers they attract. At the end of the trial period, the aspiring reporters were then hired or let go on the basis of their traffic.[18]

Hamsters

In September, 2010, the *Columbia Journalism Review* cover story by Dean Starkman featured a drawing of a cute hamster on a wheel. No journalist had the slightest doubt what that referred to: journalists at news organizations were expected increasingly to produce more stories than ever before, quality be damned. Starkman wrote, "The Hamster Wheel isn't speed; it's motion for motion's sake. The Hamster Wheel is volume without thought. It is news panic, a lack of discipline, an inability to say no."[19] It has only grown worse. In 2014, The Portland *Oregonian*, long a very highly regarded daily, with

Pulitzer Prizes to its credit, asked reporters to increase the average number of posts to the website each day by 25 percent in the first half of 2014 and another 15 percent in the second half – oh, and, by the way, to "produce top-flight journalistic and digitally oriented enterprise as measured by two major projects a quarter" with specific goals for both "page views" and reader "engagement."[20]

Loss

If you have ever been a member, or even a loyal fan, of a winning team, you know what pleasure that provides. If you have ever been on a losing team – not just for a few games, but for a long and irretrievable slump of one defeat after another, you know how it colors everything for you, on and off the playing field. After a death in the family, the survivors live on, and one day – but it takes time for that day to come – they do not think of themselves as survivors first, before all else. After a fire or flood, communities mourn, regroup, rebuild. This, too, takes time. At first, people in the community live unremittingly in relation to the loss. Picture yourself, then, in a contemporary American newspaper newsroom where about a third of your colleagues from ten years ago are no longer there.[21] Nor are they being replaced. There are a lot of empty desks. You would have to go back to 1970 when the US population stood at 203 million, not the 308 million it became by 2010, to find about the same number of editorial employees in newsrooms as you do now. So, in 1970 there was one daily newspaper journalist for every 500 Americans; today there is one for every 750 Americans.

There are just fewer hands on deck trying to cover essential areas. In 2003, there were close to 500 newspaper reporters stationed in state capitals full time to report on state politics – today that number is only about 300. According to a Pew Research Center report, 164 full-time jobs have been lost in state capital newspaper reporting. No one claims that 500 was just the right number, or that with 500 the coverage of state politics reached a peak of vigor and depth. Nor is there reason to deny that the 126 new full-time statehouse reporters who work for a variety of new, primarily online, publications

(some of them "insider" newsletters, others partisan or advocacy news operations, and a variety of general news start-ups)
make up some of the gap. It is possible, in fact, that the new
digital resources allow the smaller number of statehouse journalists to collectively report better than the more populous
newsrooms did in 2003. But this is not very comforting if
you are one of the 164 who lost a job at the state capital, or
if you are one of the others who lost a colleague or friend or
competitor – or a colleague-friend-competitor.[22]

Zing!

There has been a proliferation of news genres. There have
long been a variety of types of news genres in journalism, by
no means only the inverted pyramid, fact-centered, humorless,
impersonal hard news story, untinged by irony, analysis, or
much in the way of context. That conventional story, once
dominant, made more and more room for analytical or contextual stories from the 1970s on, including what Rodney
Benson has called the "emotional first-person narrative." That
journalistic form is much more rare, he finds, in France, where
more often one can find a "debate ensemble," a set of closely
related stories on a single topic that display different facets
of the topic from different viewpoints and without a single
authorial voice that tries to coordinate them.[23] Benson criticizes
the American first-person narrative for its frequent failure to
go beyond narrative to analysis. I emphasize only that it is a
distinct genre and one that seeks not to "inform" in the conventional who-what-when-where manner, but to evoke human
identification and emotional response. It has antecedents in
journalism going back to the nineteenth century, but it grew
more prominent since the 1970s as leading newspapers sought
to provide something television rarely did, something the
increasingly college-educated population responded to.[24]

But that was just a beginning. With digital journalism,
inventing new genres and formats for presenting news – and
thereby redefining it – became an irresistible pursuit for journalists, independent writers, technologists, and all the blurred
combinations of identities at work in news today. When *New
York Times* executive editor Bill Keller, in 2005, announced

the integration of the print and online newsrooms, he looked forward to reorganizing "our structures and our minds" and to making a new journalism "in forms that are familiar and yet-to-be-invented."[25] In 2010, *Guardian* editor Alan Rusbridger enthused: "Journalists have never before been able to tell stories so effectively, bouncing off each other, linking to each other (as the most generous and open-minded do), linking out, citing sources, allowing response – harnessing the best qualities of text, print, data, sound, and visual media. If ever there was a route to building audience, trust, and relevance, it is by embracing all the capabilities of this new world, not walling yourself away from them."[26]

Search

"Search is the watchword of the information age," sociologist David Stark has written. "Among the many new information technologies that are reshaping work and daily life, perhaps none are more empowering than the new technologies of search."[27] David Carr was right. Online searching is more efficient than newsroom hunt and peck. More information is available online, more and more of which turns out to be just a few clicks away. If there had been no recessions and no Craigslist, news organizations would still have cut some thousands of jobs – because they could. They could put out the news at the same or better quality with many fewer people in the newsroom.

At the same time, "search" can be gamed. It can be manipulated by a variety of techniques known collectively as "SEO" or "search engine optimization." What, the SEO specialist asks, leads the algorithm at Google to place a given item higher or lower in the list it retrieves instantly when you enter in a string of search words? How can you write a headline or a lead sentence or how can you craft a title for a book, a song, a film, a performance to bring it to the top of the list? Or, in the businesses that seek to repair damaged online reputations, how can you push down onto the second or third or tenth page of items Google spits out that old felony or nagging old controversy with your name on it? The extraordinary abundance of information online is not presented randomly or neutrally; reporters have not escaped partiality or public relations by checking Google rather than their associates around the newsroom.

Collaboration

Online news operations and the conventional newspaper, television stations, and public radio have all moved from an ethic of exclusivity to an ethic of sharing. This has been promoted especially by the small, online, often nonprofit news organizations that are rarely "destination" websites. They need and use other media to get their stories out and to get their names into circulation. The editors of one of the first online-only news nonprofits, Voiceofsandiego.org, appear regularly on commercial television and public radio in San Diego to disseminate their work. It is advertising and public service rolled into one. Newspapers that once would have done everything in their power to avoid crediting a competitor or even mentioning a competitor now trade news-gathering tasks with former rivals, mention the bloggers they read, accept stories from ProPublica, collaborate with Kaiser Health Fellows, take stories from education reporters at the Hechinger Institute at Columbia Teachers College, or work on investigative projects with the California Healthcare Foundation journalism program at the University of Southern California. Students in former *Boston Globe* reporter Walter Robinson's seminar at Northeastern University publish front-page investigative reports in the *Globe*.[28]

Data

Newly available relevant data make first-class journalism more accessible than ever before. You do not have to be the *New York Times* with a newsroom of 1,000 to go online and find out which foreign lobbyist contacted which members of Congress regarding which bills; you just go to www.foreign.influenceexplore.com, a website produced and maintained by an open-government nonprofit, the Sunlight Foundation, collaborating with the online investigative journalism nonprofit ProPublica. News organizations today produce not only news stories, but also databases.

If you are a reporter interested in the topic of congressional "earmarking" of bills, how do you pursue it? You go to the website of Taxpayers for Common Sense, a conservative-leaning nonprofit founded in 1995, that has compiled and keeps updated an "earmarking" database that has become the starting point for Washington reporters on the "earmark" trail.

You want to report on your local congressional delegation's voting record? This was until recently a time-consuming task. US government online records did not make it possible to download roll-call votes by the name of the legislator. You could go online for every bill that came for a vote and scroll down and find Representative Smith and keep a tally on your own, but you could not search for "Representative Smith" and get the good congressman's voting record for each bill. But now you can do exactly that at OpenCongress.org or GovTrack.us (both constructed by nonprofit open-government organizations) or WashingtonPost.org.

Great claims have been made for this new transparency, but old Washington hands see drawbacks to it: how can politicians risk the deals and the compromises that make politics work when their every move is visible to the press and the public? Champions of privacy also worry. So do journalists themselves, who recognize the legitimate needs of vulnerable individuals, some of whom bravely put themselves at risk by serving as sources for reporters and passing on inside information. The rise of transparency practices from the Freedom of Information Act (1966) on to e-government initiatives has proved a bounty to reporters who can research stories – or even discover stories – at their desktops or laptops. (As for those who study journalism in the academy, no universities or news organizations or professional associations of news organizations have ever produced data and data analysis about journalism itself that can compare with what the Pew Research Center provides freely to anyone who comes to their website.)

Passion

The proliferation of blogs, nonprofits, small and scrappy specialized or "single-subject" online news organizations, obsessive-compulsives, geeks, nerds, and insomniacs equipped with endless enthusiasm are all making the present digital news system operate much better than it has any right to. Journalists, along with poets, artists, musicians, actors, and dancers, have long pursued their careers without a business model, waiting tables while waiting for a break. Some journalists have set up alternative weeklies, while others have worked for political magazines or started vegetarian newsletters or pieced together a living as freelance foreign correspondents. They have lived on little income and less glory, fueled by passion, lowered expectations for comfort, and, sometimes, subsidies from parents or spouses or, today, Kickstarter. To observe this is not to recommend it, but to recognize an irrepressible force that sustains news. It burns out in many individuals as they get older, start families, aspire to own a home, seek day-to-day stability. But as journalism loses some of these people, younger people replace them with adrenalized online know-how, writing talent, and a feel for what's happening.

Participation

Citizens have long called in "tips" to news organizations. It is vastly easier to do that now. This does not mean that we can just declare journalism democratized, every man and woman their own news organization. But nor can this new broadly distributed capacity be ignored. The responsibility for maintaining society has long been shared by both full-time professionals and part-time amateurs. "Primary care" physicians are misnamed – they have long been secondary care medical practitioners. Mothers (and occasionally fathers) are society's front-line medical providers. That does not diminish the necessity for trained medical personnel, but it does mean there is a division of labor that deserves recognition and attention. In journalism, now more than ever.

Conclusion

These are some of the key features of how news gets produced in today's news organizations, for better and for worse. Once the news is produced, it seeks and frequently reaches an audience through all the old ways plus the internet. The advantages to this are so overwhelming that one has to be fairly imaginative to think of what's wrong about having news products from all over the country and from all over the world available to anyone with a computer or smart phone. That "anyone" is not yet "everyone" and will not be so for decades to come, if ever – but it already includes some billions of people.

There *are* negatives in this. People do not absorb as much when reading online as they do when reading words on paper. Having all of that easily accessible information at our fingertips is distracting. Students in college classrooms who are ostensibly using laptops for note-taking are more likely to be ordering lunch, buying movie tickets, answering email, surfing the web, or registering for a different class so they don't have to stick with this one. In the old days, of course, people doodled or daydreamed. Still, there is now some good evidence from psychological studies that even if students are actually taking notes on their laptops, they are learning less by doing so than if they had taken notes by hand on paper.[29]

But what, in the end, *should* one feel about all this? Would whistling a happy tune be whistling in the dark?

Imagine yourself as coming into journalism with high ideals and high hopes, and at a moment – the 1970s or 1980s or even the 1990s – when conventional news organizations, although slowly declining in numbers, prosper and seem permanent fixtures. Even as cities with two or three or more daily newspapers became increasingly cities with a single daily newspaper, the survivors showed very high profit margins. The journalism they produce seems to only grow richer and more varied. Yes, it includes conventional inverted pyramid just-the-facts journalism, but much more. Now some resources are set aside for investigative reporting projects. Now there is appreciation for interpretive or analytical news where journalists can inform readers about the context for the news event at hand. There is more room for personal style in, say, narratives of individuals from various walks of life designed to humanize communities or social problems, and there is advocacy as well as analysis on the "op-ed" page as well as on the editorial page. Journalism is opening up.

The legacy media were in a position to contribute to democracy, as Clay Shirky deftly put it, by virtue of a happy accident

– that advertisers were willing for their own purposes to pay for quality journalism, that "Wal-Mart was willing to subsidize the Baghdad bureau."[30] This is so, but remember how little serious accountability or watchdog journalism most American newspaper ever undertook. Or, to put it another way, how many of the 1,350 daily newspapers in this country ever had a Baghdad bureau or, before that, a Saigon bureau or a Moscow bureau – or any foreign bureau? How many fielded a full-time statehouse reporter – ever? In all of the 1,350 (or at one time 1,700) daily newspapers, Wal-Mart or, before Wal-Mart, Sears and Penny's, Nordstrom's and Macy's, A&P and Safeway, and the hundreds of thousands of car dealers, realtors, and roommate-seekers, subletters, sellers of used bikes, cars, furniture, and clothing who would later flock to Craigslist between them provided the financing that could have beefed up serious, aggressive reporting. In fact, at most profitable newspapers, this did not happen.

That said, many of the reporters who came of journalistic age in the 1970s into the 1990s had good jobs, often comradeship on the job, generally acceptable salaries, and psychic compensation in growing expectations for what journalism could and should be. In the post-Watergate era, reporters could hold their heads high in a new way.

And then the whole damn thing came crashing down. And if you were lucky enough to hold onto your job, it was a more miserable job in many ways than it had been before (see above – Clicks, Hamsters, etc.) and a more painful one (see above – Loss). What is there to feel except frustration?

Step back for a moment to the 1970s. What happened to newspapers in the 1960s and 1970s was powerful, but it had little to do with technological change. What happened was the unleashing of American journalists from complacency. It was part of a larger social transformation. What the 1960s taught many Americans, as well as countless others around the world, was not just that the government cannot be trusted, but that it is safe and perhaps admirable to say so. And say so they did, in declining assent in public opinion polls to statements like "I trust the government to do what is right" or "the government acts in the public interest most of the time" – and in letters to the editor, and votes against incumbents, and in the organizing of new associations, or in discovering or inventing new avenues for protest. A more inclusive, more noisy, more irreverent society emerged, one more comfortable with open dissent.

This is visible everywhere today – in social science, in the humanities, in journalism, in investigative reporting, in social movements, in advocacy think-tanks, in advocacy-style litigation. While reporting as such remains highly concentrated among professional journalists, a newly democratized witnessing proliferates, thanks to the power of cellphone cameras in documenting the world and occasionally changing it, and thanks to web-based sites for transmitting the documentary evidence of the witnessing, like YouTube.

It is also hard to ignore the inventiveness of some traditional news organizations in blending new media and old. Not only do reporters themselves blog on the websites of their own "old" news organizations, but they benefit from reading blogs – and they say so, citing blogs as sources in their stories. In 2008, there was an obituary in the *New York Times* for Doris Dungey. What led *The Times* to devote some of its precious print space to a death notice for Ms Dungey? She was a middle-aged blogger in Ohio – by 2008, there were millions of bloggers, so why her? Because this woman with a college degree in literature had worked in the mortgage banking business for 20 years and began blogging (on the blog "CalculatedRisk") with such skill and sass that she attracted the attention of economists of considerable note, not least of them Nobel Prize economist and *New York Times* columnist Paul Krugman, who cited her in his column. Others, less expert, just liked reading her. One grateful reader wrote after her death: "I didn't even care about mortgages when I stumbled across her writing, and to tell you the truth, the only reason I care now was because it gave me a chance to read her writing."[31]

Even if there is a paperless, or at least a paper-scarce, newspaper future just a few decades ahead, it will require a substantial financial investment to support the time-consuming, painstaking, and occasionally lawyered professional journalism that a monitory democracy requires. User-generated content or independent blogs or news dissemination by social media or any of the growing number of other remarkable and absorbing new developments in journalism – even all of them together – cannot replace the likes of the *New York Times* or the

Washington Post or the Associated Press. *The Times*, the *Post*, and the AP are of course in the midst of reinventing, if not replacing, themselves.

The original reporting that is at risk as newspapers lose readers and newsrooms shed jobs feeds the rest of the new forms of journalism, but it is also fed by them. WikiLeaks, for reasons of its own, brought together major news organizations for a cooperative publishing venture; rival news operations across the country now cooperate with one another when just a decade ago such behavior would not have been tolerated. Online nonprofits like ProPublica, the best funded and best known of them, give away the products of their investigative reporting to traditional on-paper newspapers so that word will get out. In an association called the Investigative News Network, established in 2009, 100 member organizations, almost all of them small and almost all of them begun after 2000 – do not make up for the loss of 20,000 newspaper newsroom jobs in the previous decade.[32] Still, these mostly small organizations are dedicated primarily to investigative reporting or "accountability journalism," as no conventional newsrooms ever were. They are finding ways to make the best of new technologies and new opportunities without giving up the professional dedication that has sometimes, over the long century of its emergence as a professional pursuit, made journalism worth our highest regard.

Part III
Short Takes on Journalism and Democracy

8

Citizenship – According to "The Simpsons"

This essay overhauls what began as a lecture I presented in Copenhagen in 2005, published in Denmark in 2006 in Tidsskriftet Politik. It is organized as a brief summary of the main theme and argument of my book *The Good Citizen: A History of American Civic Life* (Free Press, 1998). Any reader who wants a fuller account with all the footnoting should go to the book. You will not find any reference to The Simpsons there, but you will find the four eras of American civic life here identified as the eras of Marge, Homer, Lisa, and Bart respectively, carefully described and documented.

Understanding the role of journalism in democracy, or its impact on any of democracy's vital institutions, requires first that we understand democracy, and that we recognize that no single democracy is "generic," but a specific brand with features peculiar to a particular society with its own particular history. Moreover, the character of democracies has changed over the course of their modern emergence from the eighteenth and nineteenth centuries to the present. In the American case, which is my focus here, the character of democracy changed dramatically on at least three occasions – changes sufficient to alter profoundly not only the practices of political speech and political participation but also the very ideals of what speech and participation in a good society ought to be.

Four different eras in American political history have called forth contrasting ideals of what democracy should be and what a citizen in a democracy ought to be like. A group of high school teachers in a summer workshop I was teaching some years ago suggested to me that my position on this topic could be nicely summarized by using *The Simpsons* as a point of reference. Each of the eras of American civics ideals can be represented by a different member of the Simpson family.

The Marge Simpson Era, 1789–1820: The Deferential Citizen in Elite-Dominated Democracy

The colonial era through the Washington and Adams administrations and a bit beyond held to a model of what I call the "deferential citizen." The ideal citizen in this era was a person who recognized the leaders of the community and voted for them, deferring on any specific issue to their judgment. Picture Marge Simpson. She is kind, conscientious, and moral, but normally she "knows her place" – to be deferential, notably to her husband Homer. In the 1700s, voter turnout was low, campaigning was discouraged, voters were supposed to measure candidates in terms of their character and social standing rather than their political ideas, and voluntary organizations were welcome in private life but regarded with suspicion if they ventured positions on public affairs.

Imagine yourself a voter in colonial Virginia, where George Washington and Thomas Jefferson and James Madison learned their politics. As a matter of law, you must be a white male owning at least a modest amount of property to be eligible to vote. Of this group, turnout on election day was 40–50 percent in the 1780s. Voting was required by law and there were substantial fines for not voting – though the law was rarely enforced. If you chose to vote, your journey to vote could take several hours, since there might only be one polling place in a county. You might spend the night at the county seat. If this was George Washington's district, there might be supper and a ball at his Mount Vernon estate, with spirits flowing freely. During an election in 1758, Washington provided an estimate quart and a half of liquor per voter. As you approach the courthouse or other station where the voting is to take place, you see the sheriff supervising the affair, flanked by the candidates for office.

You step up to the sheriff, announce your vote in a loud voice, audible to all those around you, and then you go over to the candidate you have voted for and shake hands in a ritual of social solidarity. Your vote has been an act of assent, restating and reaffirming the social hierarchy of a community in which no one but a local notable would think of standing for office. Voting is conducted entirely in public. Voters are ritually rewarded by the gentlemen they have favored.

In such a world, what information did a voter require? Colonial education aimed to instill religious virtue, not to encourage competent citizenship. Schooling and reading were understood to be instruments inducting citizens more firmly into the established order; any notion of an "informed citizen" was simply not a leading idea for the founders' sense of politics. The whole of the citizens' informational duty was to learn enough of the candidates' characters to turn back the ambitious and self-seeking at the polls, not to learn enough to evaluate public issues themselves – that was a job for the elected representatives.

The Homer Simpson Era, 1820s–1890s: The Party-Loyal Citizen in Party-Dominated Democracy

In the early 1800s, as mass-based political parties emerged to replace the party-phobic world of the founders, the ideal citizen shifted from the deferential man of property to the democratic, enthusiastic, party-affiliated participant. A liberal and decidedly elitist regime, to graft a contemporary term onto it, began to be liberal *and* democratic. Where the founders frequently spoke of "democracy" with distaste and understood themselves to be the builders of a "republican" form of government that would accommodate but not surrender to forms of popular rule, the term "democracy" was held aloft as a banner and appeared to sweep all before it. Modes of civic participation multiplied, as did the varieties of people welcomed into the political field. Of the new participatory organizational forms – from democratized churches to temperance reform associations to abolitionist clubs – the political party became the central avenue of political engagement. Parties involved masses of citizens in local and regional nominating conventions, and many more in the picnics, barbecues, torchlight processions, "pole raisings," glee clubs, brass bands, hooliganism, and mass mobilization on election day.

This festive politics proved remarkably sturdy and popular for most of the nineteenth century. Homer Simpson would have fit right in, especially with so much of the election day activity centering as much in drinks at the party's favorite taverns as in the act of voting itself. The deferential citizen receded and, to a large extent, was replaced by the enthusiastic citizen, the partisan citizen, someone participant in the festive election campaign. On election day, tens of thousands of workers were hired by the political parties to stand near the polling place and hand out party "tickets." Voters would take a ticket from one of these "ticket peddlers" – obviously, one offering tickets for their preferred party. They would then proceed to the ballot box to deposit their ticket. Voters did not even need to look at their ticket. They did not mark it in any way – clearly, literacy was not required. Very often, once the ticket had been deposited, the voter received payment for his effort. In New Jersey in the 1880s, as many as one-third of the electorate expected payment for voting, usually an amount between one and three dollars.[1] It is not a surprise that this was the era of the highest voter turnout in American history, with 70–80 percent turnout (excluding the South) common.

What did these votes express in those days? James Bryce, a British scholar and statesman who served for some years as Britain's Ambassador to the United States, wrote in 1888 that he asked of the leading American political parties: "What are their principles, their distinctive tenets, their tendencies? Which of them is for free trade, for civil service reform, for a spirited foreign policy?" And he answered his own question this way:

This is what a European is always asking of intelligent Republicans and intelligent Democrats. He is always asking because he never gets an answer. The replies leave him in deeper perplexity. After some months the truth begins to dawn upon him. Neither party has anything definite to say on these issues; neither party has any principles, any distinctive tenets.[2]

Modern historians agree. Political historian Paula Baker writes: "Party politics in this period may be considered only marginally political, in the sense that it lacked a direct connection with government or policies."[3]

This is the foundation for the highly energized and superficially politicized world of nineteenth-century American politics. The question of who votes or how many people vote cannot be separated from the question of what voting means. A far greater proportion of eligible voters went to the polls in presidential elections than they typically do today, but why was that? Think of these voters as so many Homer Simpsons. Typically, they did not vote out of strong conviction that one party offered better policies than others; parties tended to be more devoted to distributing offices than to advocating policies. Loyalty to a party was more about comradeship than policy, more an attachment than a choice, something similar to a contemporary loyalty to a football team. Voting choices were more about affiliation than conviction. Drinks, dollars, and drama brought people to the polls, and, more than that, social connection, even "identity politics" if you will, but rarely ideas or programs.

The Lisa Simpson Era, 1890s–1920s: The Informed Citizen in a Party-Wary Democracy

The period 1890–1920 brought a flock of important political reforms, unmatched anywhere else in the world for their hostility to the power of parties and the enthusiastic and theatrical mode of civic participation the parties sponsored. State-printed ballots listing candidates of all eligible political parties became the norm, rather than party-printed tickets listing only the party's candidates; nonpartisan municipal elections in some cities replaced machine-dominated urban party politics; the initiative and referendum and the direct election of senators weakened the party as the link between citizen and state;

party-subsidized and party-directed newspapers gave way to an independent-minded commercial press. All these developments provided the institutional groundwork for a new citizenship ideal, the ideal of an informed citizen.

This informed-citizen model was well suited to single-issue and policy-oriented interest groups, from the Grand Army of the Republic and its advocacy of veterans' pensions, to the women's suffrage movement. In fact, in the wake of helping to achieve women's suffrage, the League of Women Voters emerged as a leading voice of information, informed policy discussion and debate, and modes of civic engagement intentionally at arm's length from party politics.

It was the sort of civic model that would make Lisa Simpson proud. It saw a move in the parties themselves to a more "informational" or "educational" style of campaigning, as historian Michael McGerr called it.[4] The political parties did not die, but the Progressive Era's distaste for the nineteenth-century mode of politics successfully promoted a new ideal of a rational, issue-centered citizenry. Political parades still took place in 1900 and 1904, a vestige of the old ways, but they were rapidly dying out. By 1908, the occasional parade was described as "simply a curiosity, a pale reminder of an earlier time."[5] Banner-raisings and pole-raisings tapered off. The parties stopped hiring glee clubs and brass bands for rallies, and published pamphlets instead.

As parties invested less in rallying their own loyal followers and moved to persuading uncommitted voters, policy-oriented moral entrepreneurship found a new place. If party loyalty could be sustained by Fourth of July rhetoric, the promise of jobs, and social pressure on election day, party success in the new era turned to party programs that promised good policies more than government jobs. The changes in political campaigning were part of a whole family of reforms that altered political communication profoundly. People now had to register to vote. Election fraud became more difficult. Bribery declined. Newspapers became less partisan and a new emphasis on informed voters by the 1920s led some states, particularly in the west, to provide printed information guides for all voters. In states like California and Oregon today, these guides are produced at government expense and can be hundreds of pages long.

Ballot reform epitomized the new politics. Adopted almost everywhere in a few short years in the 1890s, supported by labor as well as by upper-class genteel reformers, the so-called "Australian ballot" adopted a new way of voting, taken from a mid-nineteenth-century reform in Australia. In this move from party-distributed tickets that the voter simply placed in the ballot box to state-provided ballots that voters marked, the center of political gravity symbolically shifted from party to voter. Not incidentally, underlining the Lisa Simpson model of citizenship, one now needed basic literacy to mark a ballot. Voting changed from a social and public duty to a private right, from a social obligation to the party enforceable by the social pressure of party workers around the polling place to a civic obligation or abstract loyalty, enforceable only by private conscience, as voters marked their ballot in the privacy of a voting booth. The "informed citizen" ideal imposed more challenging cognitive tasks on prospective voters than ever before. It constituted the language by which Americans still typically measure political virtue. At the same time, with the "informed citizen" newly enshrined, there was a new mechanism – literacy tests – for disenfranchising African Americans and immigrants and a new tradition of handwringing over popular political ignorance.

Historian Richard D. Brown has traced the idea of an informed citizenry in America from 1650 to the Civil War. Although he found glimmers of the idea as early as the mid-1500s in England, it was not well developed and certainly did not dominate. Even the Glorious Revolution's Bill of Rights in 1688 guaranteed freedom of speech only in Parliament, not outside it. In Britain and its American colonies the education of gentlemen was favored, but not that of the general population. Where charity schools were established to educate the common people, the object was to teach them "to value subordination and deference over the siren call of demagogues."[6] Until at least the 1760s, the idea of an informed citizenry remained "inconsequential" and the founding fathers' praise of the wide diffusion of knowledge and a free press had a "ritualized" ring to it.[7] The American founders advocated an informed citizenry as a defensive gesture, urging knowledge to safeguard against demagoguery but rarely defining what positive knowledge citizens ought to acquire. In the early nineteenth century, informing citizens became a task for advancing a disciplined and productive workforce, for assimilating immigrants to American life, and for cultivating law-abiding citizens, but not for equipping voters to vote intelligently. That would not be emblazoned on American hearts and minds until the very end of the nineteenth and beginning of the twentieth century.

The Bart Simpson Era, 1950s to Today: The Irreverent Citizen in Trans-Electoral Democracy

And Bart? What does Bart Simpson represent? Bart is the anti-authoritarian, individualist, irreverent, rights-claiming citizen of the era ushered in by the civil rights movement. It is tempting to see him as an anti-citizen but, instead, he offers another ideal-type figure of what good citizenship looks like.

To some degree, Bart simply plays pure id to Lisa's pure superego, his impulse to her conscience, but there's something more than this in Bart. Like the representatives of so many of the liberation movements that have powered American politics since Rosa Parks refused to relinquish her seat to a white man on a bus in Montgomery, Alabama in 1955, Bart asserts his rights. This may be aggressive or defiant, or it may be self-serving, but to claim a right is not merely to grab what you want. It is an implicit agreement to make a case on the basis of common principles, common aims, and common laws. For most social movements – be they pro-life or pro-choice, environmentalist or advocating living wage ordinances, in support of a patients' bill of rights or of school choice – the politics of the past 60 or 70 years has increasingly operated through mechanisms on the fringes of the political parties and not always readily linked to them. Social movements have spawned a bewildering array of political approaches as they have enlarged – exploded – the arena of politics itself. Political scientist Robert Dahl observed in 1961 that most people have little interest in politics as such; their concerns are not about politics but are about "food, sex, love, family, work, play shelter, comfort, friendship, social esteem, and the like."[8] Since 1961, however, every one of these areas has been politicized. This is Bart's world, not entirely serious or sober or responsible, but playful and brash and irreverent, sometimes charming and sometimes crude or gross, breaking with convention.

The Bart Simpson era of citizenship is in part about rights, in part about the expressiveness of the protests for those rights, including sit-ins and mass demonstrations. It includes expletives, such as the jacket worn by Robert Paul Cohen in a Los Angeles courthouse in 1968 on which the words, "Fuck the Draft," were printed. It includes the high school students in Des Moines, Iowa in 1969, who were suspended for wearing black armbands in school to protest the Vietnam War. Cohen sued for his First Amendment right to free speech, ultimately taking his case to the Supreme Court, where he won. The young people in Des Moines did likewise, and also won their case. What makes them part of the Bart Era is the irreverence, chutzpah, and theatricality of their claims on the public's attention. This era features also the cantankerous, isolated, stubborn leadership of a Ralph Nader or the perhaps money-grubbing but certainly stubborn and dedicated lawyers who represented clients for years in suits against tobacco companies. It includes the likes of Cindy Sheehan, the mother of Casey Sheehan, a 24-year-old soldier who died in the Iraq War in 2004. Ms. Sheehan kept a vigil outside George W. Bush's ranch in Crawford, Texas for weeks in the summer of 2005 while the president was vacationing there. Although she failed in her attempt to meet the president in person, she succeeded in inspiring scores of others to join her in Crawford, including other mothers of soldiers killed in Iraq.

Maggie Simpson's Future: Is There a New Model Citizenship Emerging?

Who or what does Maggie Simpson represent? What model of citizenship will she embody as she grows up? What view or views of citizenship and politics will she claim for herself?

Maggie, like other citizens of the future, will borrow from the four models already described – none of them, not even deferential citizenship, has disappeared. The later models are overlays on the former. I think it can be said, though, that the informed citizen model dominates the imagination of scholars, of political activists, of school teachers, and other civic educators. Deference as a model is entirely repressed, enthusiastic partisanship feels too much like an abdication of independent thought to be warmly embraced, and the combination of rights-oriented citizenship with irreverence in pursuing rights is still identified as an alternative model of civic participation, a counter-current rather than a fully realized new form in itself.

Most speculation about a future of citizenship centers on the impact of new media on politics, but too much of this discussion appears sterile and thin. It is easy to see that virtual social networks established through new media provide novel opportunities for both political expression and political mobilization. New media serve political activism; new social movements make use of new technologies – but then, who doesn't?

Suppose you want to demonstrate not that new technologies were a source of energy for the Arab Spring (if anyone still recalls that brief, hopeful moment) or for Occupy Wall Street (ditto), but that new technologies have so far had minimal impact on democracy. You can show that social networking preceded new technologies – and, of course, it did; or you can show that powerful institutions use new media to greater effect than resource-poor social groups, and this is also true; or that politics-as-usual remains largely untouched by new technologies. It is difficult to see how President George W. Bush's Iraq policy or President Obama's – or Germany's or France's or Britain's or Israel's or Saudi Arabia's – were altered by new information technologies. In fact, this is so preposterous a notion that no one, so far as I know, has seriously suggested it. Of course, the leakiness of communication in an era of email has embarrassed governments, with the human rights violations carried out by US personnel in the prison of Abu Ghraib in Iraq in the early 2000s being an early example. In that case, the technological factor was digital photography; it briefly embarrassed the Bush administration and more enduringly emerged as a symbol of American indifference to world opinion. But responses to Abu Ghraib, and to the infringement of civil liberties at the US detention camp at Guantánamo Bay, have taken place in the usual congressional committees and courtrooms, both military and civil, in just the way they used to, cable TV or not, internet or not. WikiLeaks, former US soldier Chelsea Manning's wholesale leak, as well as that of former CIA employee Edward Snowden, have all had a brief impact on how foreign policy is conducted and how carefully diplomatic communications are protected, but they failed to keep Secretary of State Hillary Clinton from using an unsecured private server for confidential communications. How did the public come to learn about Clinton's email communications? From the original news reporting of a legacy news organization, the *New York Times*, willing and able to invest in the kind of labor-intensive reporting it has long been recognized for.

If there is any kind of new politics that has been disproportionately enabled by new communication technologies, it is probably international terrorism, not democracy. Could Al Qaeda and, later, ISIS have worked anything like so well without email and mobile phones? Could decentralized guerilla groups coordinate with one another around the globe and recruit new members without these modern forms of communication? It is plausible to argue that the decentralized, global, and clandestine character of international terrorism finds the internet a particularly congenial medium.[9]

But has the practice of engaged citizenship found a new model, a new set of "shoulds" and "should nots" in encouraging good citizenship, a new array of forms and genres of political participation suitable for a more intensely networked world? A world where people can easily blow off political steam in brief moments, gather information about politics more efficiently, occasionally take actions or make quips that reach large audiences without having had to present them face-to-face to anyone; where political campaigns may expertly raise funds or test slogans, where terrorist organizations and legitimate voluntary organizations may recruit effectively, and where complete bullshit crosses one's computer screen more readily than ever before?

Something new is afoot, to be sure. Whether it takes us into a new era is another question. The telegraph made a difference in news-gathering and news transmission, but it did not catapult the world into new modes of citizenship. The same can be said of radio. Arguably, the same is true of television, although television in particular changed the way people get their news and remains powerful for Americans today, still being, for many, their primary news source. But did the forms and models of civic and political participation fundamentally shift?

The internet and its various entrepreneurs from Google to Facebook to YouTube have been great assets to what has been called "monitory democracy" or "counter-democracy" or even "between-elections democracy" (that is, the idea that elections are no longer the single center of democratic participation and mobilization).[10] But while I think the human production and exchange of information and the production of public knowledge has been changed more by digital communications than by any other technological shift since the printing press, I think this is but one element in the construction of whatever new models of citizenship may emerge, not the whole story. The "whole story": the very phrase is presumptuous – that there is or will be a "whole" and that it will have the coherence of a "story." I don't think that will be the case – and I do not think that is something we should regret.

9

The Multiple Political Roles of American Journalism

This essay was originally published in Bruce J. Schulman and Julian E. Zelizer, eds., *Media Nation: The Political History of News in Modern America* (2017). Does it contradict the emphasis throughout this book on the inestimable value journalists create by placing professional judgments above political commitments? No, it does not. As it tries to explain in its opening paragraphs, this essay attempts to clarify the ways in which journalism, even in news organizations dedicated to professionalism, under some circumstances makes room for politics to enter into the choices it makes.

American journalists often profess to stand outside politics. And yet they also hold that no institution is more essential to constituting democracy than the press. This is not a contradiction. An umpire or referee stands outside the game of baseball or football, soccer or basketball, and yet the games would be difficult or impossible without them – and difficult or impossible if the players or the viewers did not have faith in the referees' essential fairness and consummate professionalism.

But the metaphor of the umpire does not quite fit journalism. In sports, the responsible referee does not ever enter into the game. The responsible journalist does, sometimes. Some journalists of high professional standards and standing may even do so regularly. The professional bodies that formally or informally represent journalists may also on occasion enter into the game. The most prestigious journalists in Washington, who talk to government officials and publish information they relay, recognize that the information the source provides in an interview may be a "leak," or it may be an authorized "plant," or it may be what David Pozen has dubbed a "pleak" – something ambiguously in between an authorized plant and an unauthorized leak.[1] Reporters here are not necessarily playing the same game that the official is playing – politics – but are playing a game of their own – proving their journalistic skill and advancing their careers by publicly demonstrating intimacy with government officials. This is not necessarily politics, but neither is it "not-politics."

There is value for journalism and, I think, for democracy when journalists assert their neutrality or professionalism. But from the viewpoint of a historian or social scientist analyzing the press, there is no virtue in taking these pronouncements at face value. In a recent episode, NBC news anchor Brian Williams backpedaled from, and apologized for, his statement that in covering the Iraq war he had flown in a helicopter that was hit by RPG fire. The military newspaper *Stars and Stripes* quickly and correctly reported that this never happened and that Williams had puffed up his own risk-taking and heroism. In his apology, Williams said: "In the midst of a career spent covering and consuming news, it has become painfully apparent to me that I am presently too much a part of the news, due to my actions."[2] This is an awkward adaptation of the self-defining, self-protecting, and self-legitimating trope among journalists, the distinction between "covering" news as a neutral bystander and becoming "a part of the news," a dangerous, prohibited practice. But it is not, in fact, prohibited in practice even though it is denied in professional self-presentation.

What I want to do in this chapter is to offer categories of instances when journalists enter into political activities they claim to stand apart from. These are important elements in what journalists do, but I caution readers that this does not mean that professionalism does not exist. It does not mean that "objectivity" is a patently false ideology. It means that life in a democracy close to the centers of political power is very complicated, that journalists can and often do wear multiple hats at once, and that, leaving aside the occasional saint, purity of motive and action is impossible.

I am going to give a few examples here, primarily from the era since 1945, by which point an ideal of objectivity and professionalism was regnant in American journalism. If we look back to the nineteenth century or early twentieth century, politicized journalism was so much taken for granted that fastidious efforts of journalists to demonstrate their political neutrality were not a fundamental element in the image journalists projected.

This is not a general historical narrative. It is simply a list, illustrated with historical examples, of ways in which the US press has acted politically or at least has acted politically in this democracy at a particular moment.

The Press as Partisan or Advocate

This is simple, obvious, and important, and I have nothing to add to what everybody knows: almost all daily newspapers have an editorial page in which they advocate public policies, endorse candidates for office, and otherwise express opinions on public affairs that the owner of their news organization approves or, at least, does not actively disapprove.

The editorial page with its direct attempt to persuade rather than to report is a journalistic practice of long standing. It is a political intervention. And for the ideologists of professionalism in journalism, it is invariably ignored. More than ignored, it may even be shunned. Former *Washington Post* editor Leonard Downie, Jr. (a friend and sometime coauthor of mine) told me that, as executive editor, he never read his paper's editorial page. The editorial page was as much a separate department as advertising or home delivery – and Downie did not want the news pages to be inadvertently influenced by advocacy positions taken in editorials.

Journalists have also been advocates off the editorial pages, but without the same legitimacy. The opinion columnist is granted a longer leash to be a party or candidate or policy advocate, although not in the mandarin fashion of either Joseph Alsop or Walter Lippmann in the past. Those gentlemen did much more than advocate in their columns. They also advised presidents behind the scene. Lippmann was all over politics. He advised Republican presidential candidate Wendell Willkie in 1940. Also, in 1940 he worked out a plan with the British ambassador to the United States to get around isolationist opposition to providing aid to Britain; he enlisted General John J. Pershing to make the case to the public, and wrote Pershing's speech. He worked with a Roosevelt aide to draft what would become the Lend-Lease bill. And he was still at it in 1945 when he teamed up with *New York Times* correspondent James Reston to convince Republican Senator Arthur Vandenberg to abandon his well-known isolationist leanings. He and Reston wrote a speech for Vandenberg that was delivered in the Senate to great acclaim. Among those who subsequently publicly praised the speech were Reston, who wrote in a news story in *The Times* that it was "wise" and "statesmanlike," and Lippmann, who used his syndicated column to praise Vandenberg's about-face.[3]

The Press as Lobbyist

News organizations in the United States are almost all private businesses and they sometimes have important financial interests at stake in government actions. Sometimes they advocate for their business interests by, for example, testifying before Congress or arguing in the hallways of Congress for favored postal rates, or urging upon the Federal Communications Commission a ruling they believe would best serve their private financial advantage.

Sometimes the news media take positions on behalf of their professional, rather than their strictly economic, interests, and this cuts closer to matters that make journalism professionals squeamish. Here the press advocates for public policies not as corporate entities but as professional entities, and the most active effort comes not from publishers but from professional associations of working journalists.

Let me offer an extended example. The Freedom of Information Act (FOIA) became law in 1966. It became much more effective in 1974. It began with a hard-working California Congressman named John Moss. In 1953 Moss was a freshman Congressman and innocently asked the Civil Service

Commission for data on dismissals of government employees for disloyalty. He did not want names, he wanted numbers. The Civil Service Commission said no. "Well, the Commission refused to supply the information requested by the committee," Moss later recalled. "This was my first experience with an agency refusing to respond to the legitimate demands of the legislative body...It was the case of a freshman member being somewhat outraged over Executive arrogance."[4] It took a decade for the individual outrage of one man to generate collective action in Congress. This was the first freedom of information act since Sweden instituted one in 1766. It was the first in the world with significant influence. It had no public support – and no public opposition. Outside Congress, no one much cared. FOIA does not cover Congress itself, or the courts, or the President, but only the executive agencies. It became law as an effort by Congress to hold the executive to account. It is used frequently by journalists and historians, among others.

How did it pass? How did it pass when the Eisenhower, Kennedy, and Johnson administrations showed little interest in it and when, in the end, every single executive agency head who testified before Congress testified against it? It passed with the help of the news media, not in covering it but in advocating for it in the halls of Congress.

In 1955, organized groups in journalism cheered the establishment of the subcommittee on government information that John Moss chaired. James S. Pope, who had served on and chaired the American Society of Newspaper Editors' (ASNE) Freedom of Information Committee in the early 1950s, recalled that the establishment of the Moss committee came as a welcome surprise to journalism's leaders, "We had not really expected to get such political clout so early; it was like gaining a fleet of nuclear subs."[5] Moss committee staff early on consulted with James Russell Wiggins of the *Washington Post*, then head of the ASNE Freedom of Information Committee; Lyle C. Wilson, United Press vice president and Washington bureau manager; Bill Beale, Associated Press Washington bureau manager; and a dozen reporters who could testify to specific instances of government suppression of the news. Media leaders backed Moss from the beginning, and Moss encouraged their support. "I hope more of you will bring your complaints to the Subcommittee," he told a meeting of news executives in 1957. "By demanding your right of access to Federal information – and by bringing the case to the attention of the Subcommittee if your right is disregarded – you can help reverse the present Federal attitude of secrecy."[6]

The ASNE, founded in 1923, had taken no interest in government secrecy until World War II, and then only seeing it as a problem in other countries; the ASNE took it for granted that Americans could and should instruct the rest of the world in press freedom. Only as the Cold War developed did journalists become concerned about press freedom at home.

The ASNE created its first committee on freedom of information – the Committee on World Freedom of Information – in 1948. In the same year, Sigma Delta Chi, the national journalism honor society, created a Committee on Advancement of Freedom of Information – likewise, with a global, not a national, focus. The ASNE and Sigma Delta Chi both moved toward a domestic focus by 1951.[7]

A freedom of information movement also developed at state and local levels as well as at the national level – which is to say, journalists were by no means exclusively preoccupied with secrecy related to national security. A 1952 *Indiana Law Journal* article on "Access to Official Information" opens with three examples, only one of which was about national security: a New Mexico newspaper reporter was denied permission to witness a US Navy rocket testing at the White Sands, New Mexico proving grounds. The other examples were about the confidentiality of federal tax collectors' actions in levying fines on Albany, New York taverns for adulterating liquor, and Oregon's state board of education's secret meetings about separating the state university's dental school from its medical school.[8] Sigma Delta Chi, the AP Managing Editors, the ASNE, the National Editorial Association, and state press associations all promoted state open meeting and public records laws.[9]

This freedom of information movement in journalism proved a natural ally for Moss – and he was equally an ally for the movement. Sometimes "the Moss Committee staff wrote the press organizations' freedom-of-information annual reports – which were in turn widely reproduced in the press in terms laudatory of the Moss Committee."[10] The committee's investigations were organized in consultation with key leaders in the press and Moss employed a staff dominated by former newspaper reporters, including chief of staff Sam Archibald, a former *Sacramento Bee* reporter. Moss spoke all over the country – often to journalism schools and press associations. Journalists testified before his committee and offered him useful examples of government suppression of the news.[11]

Media scholar Jim Carey wrote, in one of his last publications, that journalists are obliged to abandon their objectivity in exactly this domain: "[They] can be independent or objective about everything but democracy. About democratic institutions, about the way of life of democracy, journalists are not permitted to be indifferent, nonpartisan, or objective. It is their one compulsory passion, for it forms the ground condition of their practice."[12] American journalists and journalism organizations had come to the same conclusion in practice, if not in theory, 50 years before Carey wrote those words. This chapter in the history of American journalism is, as Carey intimates, inconsistent with general professions of political detachment, but it needs to be incorporated into how we think about the institution of journalism in democracy.

The Editor as National Security Executive

American journalists act in ways that express obligation to and affiliation with the nation-state. When they have their hands on a story they think may reveal secrets that bear on national security, they customarily notify the government ahead of publication and even negotiate the content of the story with the White House, Defense Department, or other relevant agencies. This was the case when the *New York Times* learned of the impending Bay of Pigs invasion of Cuba by the CIA in 1961 and voluntarily modified its story at the strenuous urgings of the White House.[13]

The same thing happened in 1986 when the *Washington Post* learned of a secret US underwater mechanism code-named "Ivy Bells," which had successfully tapped Soviet cable communications. The *Post* also knew that the operation had been compromised by Jack Pelton, a low-level technician for the National Security Agency (NSA) who sold information to the Russians. Newsroom executives at the *Post* met with NSA

Director Lieutenant General William Odom, who urged them not to publish anything. Odom contended that any story about Ivy Bells would be dangerous to the country, revealing to the Soviets something they did not know.

But, editor Ben Bradlee objected, Pelton spilled the beans, the Soviets already know about Ivy Bells! Nevertheless, General Odom responded, which Soviets know? There might have been internal Soviet secrecy. There might have been a cover-up. A story in the *Post* would set off a general alarm in the Soviet Union, building pressure for the Soviets to increase anti-espionage measures. Odom's protest was cogent enough to give the *Post* pause. Successive drafts were written, each less detailed than the one before. Bradlee repeatedly asked his colleagues, "What is this story's social purpose?" In the end, the *Post* published the story – over the objections of the administration – after a back-and-forth that went on for months.[14]

The *Post* made similar decisions in 2009 when longtime investigative reporter Bob Woodward received a copy of a confidential report produced by General Stanley McChrystal about the war in Afghanistan. The *Post* informed the Pentagon and the White House about what was coming. The secretary of defense, the national security advisor, and vice chair of the Joint Chiefs of Staff each asked the *Post* to reconsider. Editor Marcus Brauchli, speaking of the incident later, observed proudly that, in the American system, the government could ask, but not command, the paper not to publish; the decision was in the end the editor's, not the government's.[15]

In these cases, and many others, editors for commercial news organizations voluntarily assume the mantle of secretaries of defense, acting – ultimately on their own – as stewards of public safety.

In 2003, Dean Baquet, then managing editor at the *Los Angeles Times*, before becoming executive editor of the *New York Times*, was involved in a decision about whether to publish a damaging story about Arnold Schwarzenegger, then a leading gubernatorial candidate in California. The paper had gathered half a dozen credible allegations by women in the movie industry that Schwarzenegger had sexually harassed them. With the story ready to print just days before the election, the editors wondered if they should delay running it until after the election. Would the article not seem to be a "hit piece" sprung on Schwarzenegger? Would the timing not make it difficult for him to respond? Baquet later told a reporter (after the *LA Times* went ahead and published the story): "Sometimes people don't understand that to not publish is a big decision for a newspaper and almost a political act. That's not an act of journalism. You're letting your decision-making get clouded by things that have nothing to do with what a newspaper is supposed to do."[16]

Baquet's statement is a revealing and representative example of professional news ideology: journalism is journalism, not politics, and it should stick to that role. Journalism is making information public; choosing not to publish for any reason – except, in Baquet's view, insufficient journalistic quality or the possibility that publishing could endanger a life – abrogates one's professional responsibility.

That's not hogwash, but nor is it an accurate representation of what journalists do. Now that Mr. Baquet is the top editor at the *New York Times*, he surely finds himself on occasion in the same position as others before him – engaging in "almost a political act," conscientiously placing national security ahead of the journalistic responsibility to raise hell, come what may. Nowhere, to the best of my knowledge, have these dramatic and wrenching moments been reconciled with the notion of journalism's "outsider" standing. Indeed, nowhere, so far as I know, have these moments become a central part of the way US journalists discuss their own history or construct their own identity. They are just too uncomfortable and too deeply at odds with how journalists like to see themselves.

The Journalist as Government Insider

Journalists have often been employed in American government. They have been appointed to office. They have been elected to office. They have been friends and confidants of presidents. They have routinely served as press secretaries, of course, and media advisors, but they have also served in a variety of other staff roles. Collectively, the fact that journalists move into government, imbued with a professional ideology alien to most of the lawyers and others who inhabit the world of public officialdom helps orient government to keeping its publics in mind and strategizing how to appeal to them. I will highlight just one instance here. This concerns reporter Richard Conlon, who became staff director of the Democratic Study Group (DSG), a pioneering caucus in the House of Representatives. Through Dick Conlon, journalism played a key role in making Congress a more public and democratic institution. Let me go back a step.

Congress in the 1950s and 1960s was stunningly undemocratic. It was undemocratic when John Moss arrived in 1953. It was still undemocratic when Tom Foley, a Democrat from Washington arrived as a freshman in 1965. Foley recollected how Agriculture Committee chair Harold Cooley (D-NC) addressed him and other freshman members at the committee's first meeting:

> I hate and detest, hate and detest, to hear senior members of this committee, of either party, interrupted by junior members of this committee, of either party. You new members in particular will find that you will require some time, some of you months, others of you regrettably probably years, before you develop sufficient knowledge and experience to contribute constructively to our work. In the meantime, silence and attention, silence and attention is the rule for new members of this committee.[17]

From 1959 on, liberal Democrats grew more and more frustrated; despite having a majority in the Democratic Party, they could not get any initiatives past the Southern conservative committee chairmen.

By a practice dating to the first Congress, amendments to bills before the House were discussed and voted on when the House convened itself as the so-called "Committee of the Whole." All members of Congress are members of the Committee of the Whole, but the Committee of the Whole can convene with a much smaller quorum than the House in ordinary session. This affords it a great deal of flexibility. Moreover, individual votes in the Committee of the Whole normally went unrecorded. Often voting was by unrecorded "teller vote."[18] In this practice, each member of the House, one by one, walks up to a "teller" and votes. The total count – so many yeas, so many nays – then became part of the public record. What was not public is which representatives voted which way.

This meant that all votes on amendments to bills taken up in the Committee of the Whole that were defeated would be forever shielded from the public eye; constituents would never know if their representatives had supported or opposed key amendment on critical legislation if the amendments went down to defeat. Only amendments that the Committee of the Whole approved would be voted on publicly when the bill came up for final passage after the House resolved itself back into the House of Representatives.

This changed in 1970 with the passage of the Legislative Reorganization Act. That act opened up committee deliberations to the public, allowed television coverage of deliberations on the House floor, made committee votes public, and ended the unrecorded teller vote in the Committee of the Whole. What enabled these reforms to triumph? They were made possible in no small measure by the efforts of the DSG. The DSG was the first enduring, formally organized "caucus" in the history of the United States Congress, established in 1959 by Eugene McCarthy, then a representative in the House, later a Senator and in 1968 anti-war aspirant for President.

A Minnesota reporter, Dick Conlon became the full-time staff director of the DSG in 1968. He quickly turned the DSG into a crackerjack research outfit. He did so by insisting that it live up to his journalistic values – give both sides of a story, and write clearly and lucidly for people with very short attention spans – which is to say, members of Congress. The DSG fact sheets and reports and their own research on voting in Congress are brilliant pieces of analysis, summary, and condensation. Conlon was effective not only because he was a very accomplished writer himself, but because he was a perfectionist with others, too.

Liberals in the House in 1969 had begun working on procedural reforms to make the House responsive to its own liberal and moderate majority. The DSG became especially interested in ways to make the workings of Congress more publicly visible and, in particular, to make votes in the Committee of the Whole available to the press and the public. Conlon called attention in the DSG executive committee to the possibility that they could sell the procedural reforms they favored, including ending the unrecorded teller votes, by packaging them as "anti-secrecy" amendments to the pending reform bill. He thought this would attract news media interest, a notion that arose for him in a conversation with a reporter friend. In 1970, the DSG produced several brief reports on secrecy and unrecorded teller voting. Secrecy, according to one of the reports, reduces the effectiveness of the House, inhibits the press in its responsibilities, and denies the public the "information to which it is entitled in a democratic society."[19]

The DSG decided to promote its anti-secrecy amendments to the general public, believing that the topic of anti-secrecy would catch on with journalists. As Conlon recalled later:

> Secrecy was just a magic button with the press. As a trained journalist myself I know what made me salivate when I was reporting and I know that an editorial writer in particular sitting there behind a desk, frustrated as hell and not being able to get out and get at things is always railing against government secrecy and it was just the magic button that turned a shower of things on.[20]

DSG chair Donald Fraser wrote hundreds of letters to editorial page editors and columnists and he got support from the University of Missouri's Freedom of Information Center, which contacted 770 newspapers and hundreds of radio and television stations, too, to support the amendment.

DSG efforts produced results in newspaper editorials and opinion columns around the country. What the newspapers found irresistible was not simply the idea of anti-secrecy measures, but also the delicious irony that the vote to lift the veil on unrecorded voting in the Committee of the Whole would be taken by an unrecorded vote in the Committee of the Whole. One editorial or column after another delighted in the irony. It allowed the press to support an important but obscure reform and to ridicule Congress at the same time.[21] It was no accident that so many publications noticed the irony – the DSG itself told them about it in Donald Fraser's "Dear Editor" letter of June 30, 1970.[22]

Democracy is a matter of the public being oriented to government but also orienting government to the public. In orienting government to the public, journalists inside government have made a difference.

Journalism as Agenda Advocacy[23]

Partisan advocacy in print or electronic or digital journalism has a deep history. As journalism professionalized in the twentieth century and overt partisanship in the news columns became more rare, journalists nonetheless on occasion have self-consciously promoted attention to specific public issues.

Some of this is obvious and widely noted. The news media collectively embrace a "watchdog" role. They not only report on what government officials say and do but on what they promise – and whether they make good on their promises, and on what their sworn obligations are – and whether they live up to them. Academic studies offer abundant evidence that when the press covers politicians well, politicians become more responsive to public needs. (One especially convincing study of how well and how quickly different states in India respond to food shortages demonstrates that where media are plentiful and active, politicians have been more responsive than where media are scarce or supine.)[24]

If the general "public guardian" role of the press is much noted, there is less attention to acts of journalistic advocacy of specific topics a reporter or editor deems worth covering. It would be hard to deny that mainstream US news organizations today should cover the issue of same-sex marriage – the issue has been joined, in state after state, as a legitimate public controversy. But at what point did this issue, in recent memory too touchy for even many liberal Democrats to embrace (Barack Obama found it too hot to handle in his 2008 campaign for president), come to routinely command mainstream news attention?

In 1970, Philip Shabecoff, a *New York Times* correspondent, newly assigned to the Washington bureau, asked to be on the "environment" beat full time. His editors said no. When he did an occasional environment-related story, he recalls that the general response he got was, "What, another story about the end of the world, Shabecoff? We carried a story about the end of the world a month ago."[25] Did Shabecoff show the better news judgment – or was his a personal or political judgment that he placed before his news sense? Or were his editors insensitive to a major new public policy issue that required a good newspaper to rethink its priorities? And was it their news sense that was more politicized than his? How far ahead of public opinion or Washington opinion is it appropriate for a news organization to be? How far behind general opinion can it afford to be? There is no answer to these questions, only the recognition that these decisions are not made in some journalistic ivory tower but in a real world where political judgment necessarily enters.

Journalism as the Medium for the Formation of Political Culture

Journalism as a medium through which politics flows

So far, I have discussed ways in which specific reporters, editors, and organizations of reporters and editors make political choices and political decisions. But journalism also plays a political role in a far more collective fashion, shaping, constituting, coordinating, and legitimating specific ways of doing politics and specific ways of thinking about politics. It is possible to see this if we look at the changes wrought in journalism and in American public culture broadly speaking between 1960 and the end of the twentieth century.

Consider the work of Steven Clayman and his colleagues in their brilliant study of presidential news conferences, and how reporters' questions in them changed from 1953 through 2000. They found a marked increase in the aggressiveness of questions. The biggest change came in the late 1960s. While assertive questioning had both ups and downs in the 1980s and 1990s, it never dropped to the low levels of the 1950s and early 1960s. As Clayman and his colleagues conclude: "Sometime around the late 1960s, the tenor of Washington journalism began to change. A growing body of research converges in its portrayal of a shift toward increasingly vigorous and in some respects adversarial treatment of government officials, political candidates, and their policies."[26] Journalists themselves have placed so much emphasis on Watergate (1972–4) as a turning point that they sometimes forget that the big change in the news culture began before Watergate, and they rarely acknowledge at all that the growth of contextual journalism, a term I will explain in a moment, represents a much larger change in the character of news than a reallocation of effort to investigative reporting.

Today, essentially no one defends the journalism of the 1950s. Journalist Paul Duke remembered the Washington press corps after World War II as "rather sleepy" and "content to report from handouts and routine news briefings."[27] Reporters and politicians were frequently "pals," as political scientist Larry Sabato observes.[28] In 1959, veteran journalist Douglass Cater criticized "objective" or "straight" reporting and judged objectivity to be a "worn-out concept."[29] Cater urged that reporters be free "to contribute an added dimension to reporting which is interpretive not editorial journalism."[30]

Journalism moved exactly in the direction of the "added dimension" urged by Cater. Katherine Fink and I have charted the growth of what we call contextual reporting. We looked at two weeks' worth of front pages of the *New York Times*, *Washington Post*, and *Milwaukee Journal* for 1955, 1967, 1979, 1991, and 2003. Contextual reporting – a broad category that includes explanatory reporting but much more – barely turned up in our 1955 sample: just 8 percent of all front-page stories. By 1991 it represented half of what we found on the front page of all three newspapers. The notion that the news media are dominated today by "he-said-she-said" stories that write themselves is not a valid critique of leading US newspapers, nor has it been for several decades.[31]

What accounts for the change? Clayman, in trying to explain the stunning rise of a more critical and aggressive tone in the questions reporters asked at presidential news conferences, links it to a change in the culture, norms, and values of journalism.[32] The plausibility of this explanation grows when we recognize that European journalism moved at about the same time in the same direction, even without Vietnam and Watergate.[33]

This lends credence to Clayman's conclusion that a change in newsroom culture is key. But what caused *that*? My hunch is that a substantial part of the answer is that more journalists came to their work with a college education and, simultaneously, college education had become much more an education in critical thinking. Academic culture itself adopted more "adversarial" habits – not so much politically adversarial as intellectually adversarial. Students were expected to learn to "read against the text" in courses in the humanities, not simply to absorb accepted canons of high culture. And in the sciences and social sciences, students were increasingly encouraged not to memorize textbooks but to imagine themselves as fledgling scholars, moving on to a next level of insight by criticizing the assumptions, methods, or reasoning of the exemplars whose work they were assigned to read. This was especially true in the research universities and the small liberal arts colleges that dedicated themselves to the same critical ideals and to grooming students to go on to graduate education.

Historians have not yet integrated their own story – the story of higher education – into the broader history of modern American society. Like journalists, academics have come to believe their own public relations literature – that they are outsiders looking in. They – we – are insecure in thinking of our own corner of the world as having actually made a difference.

Journalism as a matrix in turning language to action

I have been puzzling over a paper by Lynton Keith Caldwell in *Public Administration Review*, published in 1963. Its title was "Environment: A New Focus for Public Policy?" In a scant 10 pages or so, Caldwell, a political scientist at Indiana University, proposed that, yes, the environment should be a focus for public policy. What puzzles me about it is that it was so well received, that it is much honored to this day, that there is a serious biography of Caldwell just published last year, and that students of Caldwell's collected his papers and published them as a volume many years later called, *Environment as a Focus for Public Policy*. No question mark.

My puzzlement is that, in my opinion, it's not a very good paper. The writing is pedestrian, at best. It is not well argued. When it offers a name for what to call this new "focus," it offers not "environmental policy" or "environmental studies," or even "ecology," but "ekistics," and, needless to say, this did not catch on. What caught on (and certainly not because

of Caldwell alone) is the first word of the title of the paper
– "Environment." It came to be the taken-for-granted watchword of a new consciousness, institutionalized in a new department that *Time* magazine inaugurated in 1969, "The
Environment." How on earth did that happen when the term
as part of public thinking simply did not exist before 1963?

Now, maybe it doesn't matter. Maybe "conservation" was
a perfectly serviceable term. But "conservation" is an action
people may take toward the natural world; "environment" is
the natural world itself. "Environment" thus shifts the focus
from human agency to, in a way, the context in which humans
make their lives as having agency of its own, its own demands,
its own vulnerabilities, its own retribution if we fail to give
it its due. With "conservation," humans look large and the
world around us small; with "environment," humans are put
in our place.

Does that make a difference? I think it does, but I cannot
show exactly how. But we do know that words matter, that
catch phrases matter, that rubrics matter, that language carves
up the world in one way and not another, and that journalists, among our leading meme-makers, matter. The linguist
Charles Hockett argued against the view that language deter-
mines how and what humans think. Instead, he suggested,
"Languages differ not in what *can* be said in them, but rather
as to what it is *relatively easy* to say in them."[34] That is one
of the best sentences I have ever come upon in the social sciences, and it has just the subtlety required for thinking about
the role of journalism in society. Journalists are in the business
of knowing what can be communicated easily. This places
them in the public business of politics. They are not there
alone. Others in the same business include the president's
speechwriters, the advertising executives and media consult-
ants employed for presidential campaigns, the directors of
topically themed films and documentaries, the writers of gags
and monologues for late night television, the makers of political satire or political polls, and other forums in which the
task of reducing the complex to the simple and the prosaic
to the memorable is pre-eminent. But journalists are near the
point of origin of the whole machinery of political language
and they often provide the primary forum in which political
language takes shape.

Journalists wear political hats. They do so sometimes avowedly (in editorials or opinion columns or as their principal objective in advocacy publications), sometimes under extreme situations that make them uncomfortable (in negotiating with the government to sometimes withhold information from the public to protect national security), sometimes as insiders or people very close to insiders in ways that they prefer not to discuss (except perhaps in memoirs), and sometimes in the course of trying to provide fair-minded and thoughtful leadership in reforming reportorial conventions to adapt to changing social norms and values, either a step behind or a step ahead of public opinion.

To acknowledge all this is not to declare it good or to declare it bad, but to declare it, plain and simple. To acknowledge this longstanding and continuing feature of how journalism operates may provide an improved foundation for sorting out what kind of political journalism, or political journalism beset by what sorts of circumstances, we should see as desirable, or as necessary, or as requiring criticism and reform.

10

Democracy as a Slow Government Movement

This chapter began life as a presentation to a conference of media scholars, political scientists, and others in Jerusalem in March 2017. More than a fragment but less than a finished work, I justify including it in a book about the place of journalism in democracy to explore further the "democracy" side of that topic. As I have indicated in the introduction and in chapter 8, a democracy is recognized by its institutions, not simply by its embrace of popular participation in governing. A democracy's signature features include provision for deliberation, for review, for revision – and a democracy should accordingly encourage in its citizens not only participation, but patience for the necessary slowness in the democratic political process.

In 1986, McDonald's planned to open its golden arches on the Spanish Steps in Rome. It did not happen. The expansion was shut down by outspoken protests. It was out of those protests that Carlo Perini started the Slow Food movement that spread around the world. And since then, there has been a growing advocacy of "slow" culture. A British sociologist published a serious article in 2014 on "The Slow University." Two Canadian professors published a widely reviewed book called – and calling for – "The Slow Professor." There are advocates of slow transportation. What has been called slow fashion advocates craft production rather than mass production, even though it takes more time. In each case, there is an argument that taking time is worth the bother. It produces something better than speeding up does.

All these movements began long after republican government was reinvented in the eighteenth century and was both advocated and very soon attacked as slow government. No one has ever said that autocracy or dictatorship operates too slowly. You just engineer a coup, you control the military, you take over the major broadcasting services, you detain, execute, or exile the top leaders you have deposed, and you get on with business. Voilà! You are governing.

Democracy, in contrast, is a slow process. People in a democracy have to learn to participate in politics in a civil way; they have to learn that civility requires patience with the slowness of the process itself. The claim for slow government, like slow food, is that decision-making invites participation, allows for marinating, and tastes better in the end.

There are multiple ways to think about the relationship between democracy and time. Dennis Thompson, for instance, has suggested that citizens in a democracy are more inclined than other people to value the present over the future: "Democracy is partial toward the present. Most citizens tend to discount the future, and to the extent that the democratic process responds to their demands, the laws it produces tend to neglect future generations." Thompson notes that this "presentism" has some virtues – "Compared to other forms of government, democracy is not disposed to sacrifice citizens or a whole generation for some distant future goal" – and he contrasts this with "utopian idealists, religious zealots, or radical revolutionaries who call for great sacrifices from the present generation to bring about even greater good for the future of mankind."[1] Democracy, on the other hand, attends to "actual citizens" and holds actual rulers accountable to them. But there are defects in this virtue, too, in that it neglects long-term disadvantages of present-day policies – long-term environmental risks or long-term population growth, for instance, that will leave future generations without essential resources.

What interests me here are assessments of time in the sense of pace. Does democratic government operate fast or slow, too fast or too slow? Are democratic citizens patient enough for the time that deliberation requires? Are they willing to pause to talk, consider, criticize? Do they, as is often said of children, dawdle? I want to suggest that democracy, as both its advocates and its critics agree, frequently operates at turtle-like speed. This may be good for us or bad for us or both good and bad, but it is in any case necessary. I want to take up four features of this time-as-pace aspect of democracy:

- political socialization takes time;
- elections take time;
- deliberation takes time;
- reason takes more time than passion and is a product of institutions rather than of individual minds.

Political Socialization Takes Time

In a democracy, the people at large are supposed to participate in guiding the decisions of the state. They do not normally make the decisions themselves but they go to the polls peri-odically to select the representatives who will make the deci-sions – or at least the representatives who will select and presumably keep an eye on those in the executive branch of government who will make the decisions. If things go well, people will feel they have a stake in the government. They will feel that the governors, having been elected, will be legiti-mate and will effectively represent the views and values and interests of the voters.

How long does political socialization take? How much time is required to learn to be a democratic citizen? There is no handbook on this for people born as citizens who grow up as citizens, attending public schools, joining in the celebra-tion of national holidays, taking in by osmosis or by explicit instruction the background assumptions of how the polity operates and what values it honors. For newcomers seeking to become citizens, there actually is (in the United States) a handbook – indeed, a primer on American citizenship and an exam to measure competence in mastering it.

Passing the citizenship test in the United States is not dif-ficult if one has acquired sufficient English language skills, but does passing the test indicate middling or better understanding of the American political system? Mastering a democratic political system cannot be done overnight. In fact, lack of political socialization is often seen to be a chief cause of the slow or failed transition to democracy from communist-ruled countries of Eastern Europe after 1989. Democratic governments were instituted, but in many cases could not be sustained. The absence of prior experience over time with democracy was crippling. It is as if a set of college students who have not grown up playing baseball are asked to play another team that has been playing the game from early childhood – the newcomers will lose. They do not know the fine points of the game even if they have read a handbook. They do not know in their muscles how to pitch, bat, catch, or throw.

With respect to time and speed or slowness, the following notions have to become part of the vocabulary of citizens.

First, democratic citizens should recognize that there is an ever-present possibility that a decision that has been made can be by legitimate means reversed, revised, amended, appealed, or abandoned.

Second, democratic citizens should know that as soon as they have elected a representative, they should regard that representative with respect but also with skepticism. They should have a democracy-enhancing suspicion that power corrupts and that absolute power tends to corrupt absolutely.

Third, democratic citizens should know that, barring corruption and undue insularity, government by representatives is better than government by the people themselves, even if the latter were practically conceivable. It is easier for people to retain skepticism of representatives, even representatives they themselves have voted for, than it is to challenge a built-in arrogance about the wisdom or the legitimacy of the people themselves. People know that individual representatives may make mistakes or may not take the public good as their objective; the general public may also not take the public good into account, only the good of the majority, or what feels good at the moment, or what seems to offer immediate advantage while discounting the good of future generations. In this respect, the argument of political theorist George Kateb is compelling: representative democracy is morally distinctive and, in most respects, morally preferable to direct democracy, not a "second best" system we resort to only because of the inconvenience of having all adult citizens participating in governmental decisions all the time.[2]

The great feature of representative democracies is not that they empower the people directly to elect their governors, but that they insist on skepticism toward the elected. They do so through limited terms of office and possibly limits to the number of terms an official may stay in office. They do so also, in some democracies, through "checks and balances" so that one branch of government may check rash or improvident acts of another practice. Democracies constrain even presidents and prime ministers by the rule of law. How a democratic public holds officials accountable is a central issue for democracies, and it is a complex matter. Expanding upon an analysis of accountability by Jerry Mashaw, I suggest there are four types of accountability: (1) political accountability through elections; (2) managerial accountability through agencies or processes of internal governmental audit, investigation, and inspection; (3) legal accountability through judicial review; and (4) public opinion accountability or societal accountability by the organs and institutions of civil society, the news media, and public opinion measurement.[3]

Elections Take Time

In elections, candidates and parties need time to present themselves to the voting public. This may be a very long time, with candidates jockeying for position in the next election the day after the last election was completed. But what is the "right" duration? When does an electoral season unfold too quickly or too slowly? Presidential campaigns in the United States in recent decades have ranged from 281 to 596 days. Some countries would find this insufferably long, and there is evidence that most voters, even during a long American election process, do not normally tune in to the campaign until its last two or three weeks. By law, Mexico limits election campaigns to 147 days. Japan's election law confines campaigning to 12 days. Canada does not legally limit the length of a campaign, but its longest campaign ran just 78 days.[4]

Deliberation Takes Time that Even Democracies Cannot Always Spare

A fully participating and fully deliberative and fully account-able democracy has never existed. But from the development of representative democracies in the eighteenth century to the present, some approximations have emerged and succeeded, in some ways better than ever today. Managerial account-ability in the United States began with the Federal Regis-ter Act of 1935, the Administrative Procedure Act of 1946, and the Freedom of Information Act in 1966. It grew again with the National Environmental Policy Act of 1970 that created the world's first system of environmental impact assess-ment and the requirement for publication of environmental impact statements before government agencies are free to move forward with projects that might have a negative impact on the environment. In 2011 the federal government produced 442 environmental impact statements, each open to public comment for 45 days. On any given day of the year there were 30–60 open EIS public comment periods.[5] It grew again in 1978 with the Inspectors General Act, and yet again with the growth and institutionalization inside news organizations of investigative reporting.[6] Still, even in the best and most accountable of democracies, occasions arise where there is agreement that secrecy must displace openness for the sake of the public good, checks and balances must be abridged for the sake of a state's survival. And under these circumstances, all – or nearly all – bets are off.

These situations call for expeditious and centralized decision-making. The general category for these situations is the term "emergency." War is the most common example. The word "dictator" comes from the Roman Republic – it was the title of the official appointed by the Senate to rule in times of emergency. At that point, there was no negative connotation to the term. Indeed, dictators were appointed frequently and their surprising feature, for those familiar only with the modern, entirely negative understanding of "dictator," is that the dicta-tor ruled only for a specified and limited term before he was obliged to return power to the Senate.

One of the greatest of difficulties for democracies is how to operate in emergencies when there is, or seems to be, a premium on making decisions quickly and without time or patience for deliberation and debate and the kinds of vetting and revising that are taken to be essential for making good decisions. It should not be surprising that in the US the National Emergencies Act (1976) is not a law that sets the rules for the president to declare a national emergency: it formalizes the power of the Congress to limit the president's authority to declare emergencies. Democracies cannot always act quickly enough if they require their normal time for participation and comment, notice and hearings, and so forth. So there must be democratic mechanisms for abrogating democracy. There must be accountable ways to insist that non-democratic rule may be declared – and that it can also be undeclared.

Giving Voice to Reason Takes Time

There is an old story about the American founders, apocryphal but worth retelling nonetheless. The story is that Thomas Jefferson, returning from France after the US Constitution was completed, told George Washington that he should not have agreed to a second legislative chamber, the Senate. "Of what use is the Senate?" he asked, as he stood before the fireplace with a cup of tea in his hand. As he waited for Washington's response, he poured some of the tea into his saucer, swirled it around a bit, and then poured it back into the teacup. Washington, observing him, replied, "You have answered your own question."

"What do you mean?" asked Jefferson.

"Why did you pour the tea into your saucer?"

"To cool it," said Jefferson.

"Just so," said Washington. "That is why we created the Senate. The Senate is the saucer into which we pour legislation to cool."

This was exactly Madison's attitude. "The use of the Senate," he wrote, "is to consist in its proceeding with more coolness, with more system, & with more wisdom than the popular branch."[7] The Senate, he wrote in Federalist 63, is "a defense to the people against their own temporary errors and delusions." There are moments when "the people, stimulated by some irregular passion, or some illicit advantage, or misled by the artful misrepresentations of interested men, may call for measures which they themselves will afterwards be the most ready to lament and condemn." For the founders, the people of Athens were subject to "the tyranny of their own passions."[8] Their ideal model was not Athens but Rome, and Madison noted that there had been no long-lived republic without a Senate.

Individuals as well as institutions seek ways to improve their decisions by slowing them down. They decide to "sleep on it," to wait until the next day to make a difficult decision. They may seek out "buyer's remorse" clauses in contracts when they purchase a high-priced product like a car. They want to be able to return recently purchased goods without penalty if they make the return within so many days. In all these respects, they recognize dangers to their well-being if they let their impulses overwhelm their reasoned judgment.

Conclusion: The dangers of slow democracy

President Barack Obama in the last days of his presidency expressed concern about the future: "And what I worry about in our politics is people getting impatient with the slowness of democracy, and the less effective Congress works, the more likely people are to start giving up on the core values and basic institutions that have helped us to weather a lot of storms." He would be leaving the White House, he said, with "really progressive policy beliefs," as always, "but I'm more conservative when it comes to our institutions. I've seen enough around the world when it comes to the results of complete revolution or upheaval that it doesn't always play out well."[9]

In the United States, at least, democracy has been oversold but underdefined. We have discussed citizenship as a system that invites and expects the full participation of citizens, locating democracy in the individual and identifying democracy with the individual's voice; we have talked also about deliberation, locating democracy in the interpersonal, in conversation; and we have identified democracy with well-informed citizens, locating it in reasoning individuals who choose representatives, or policies, or both. But few people, if pressed, would accept this as an adequate definition of a good form of governance. What is missing is an organized and reliable route for questioning the will of the majority (that may favor oppressing minorities) and the authority of the legislature or president. What political theorist George Kateb has termed the "radical chastening of political authority" is the central feature of representative democracies, and the feature that provides its "moral distinctiveness." The authority that elected persons hold is authority on a short leash – by virtue of a next election the representatives must face, by virtue of elections being contested by more than one legitimate party, and by virtue of the rule of law, to which representatives are as constrained as any other citizens, and the limitations imposed by constitutionalism, written or unwritten.[10]

If reducing democracy to popular participation does not recognize the essential role of holding power accountable between elections, and not only on election day, it also fails to honor the importance for sustaining a good life of withdrawal from the public and the political. In our journalized societies where news and news updates are with us constantly, so long as we are carrying a smart phone or within range of a screen carrying an ever-cycling CNN newscast, people have to remind themselves that it is not a sin to turn off or to turn away from the news. *New York Times* business writer Farhad Manjoo took a whole column early in 2018 to discuss how he thought he came to understand current affairs better by withdrawing for a month from getting news from anywhere except three daily newspapers on paper delivered to his home, *The Economist*, podcasts, and books. That might still be a lot for most people, but it is a starvation diet for a working reporter. Manjoo's mantra-length advice: "Get news. Not too quickly. Avoid social."[11]

Manjoo notes that he thinks his effort at reducing news addiction has made him a more attentive husband and father. Andrew Sullivan has made the point more broadly:

> One of the great achievements of free society in a stable democracy is that many people, for much of the time, need not think about politics at all. The president of a free country may

dominate the news cycle many days – but he is not omnipresent – and because we live under the rule of law, we can afford
to turn the news off at times. A free society means being free
of those who rule over you – to do the things you care about,
your passions, your pastimes, your loves – to exult in that
blessed space where politics doesn't intervene.[12]

The populist wave we see around the world is not simply
the consequence of anger, resentment, and disappointment
in the face of economic distress. It is not only the consequence
of a deep disquiet that our national identities are insecure,
threatened by transnational entities like the European Union,
by porous borders at a time of terrorism where people feel
drawn to the reassurances of building walls, by the transportation of viruses and communicable diseases through the glo-
balizing influences of travel and tourism, through the global
spread of metaphorical viruses that infect computer systems,
or where political and military conflicts give way to massive
human dislocations and refugees at every border.

These are real problems. But, on top of them, there is an
intellectual contribution to populism that grows from the
political theory equivalent of pop psychology. This is the
repeated saccharine rhetoric, election day editorial, schoolbook
civics lesson, and presidential pieties invoking the magical
terminology of "civic participation" or even "participatory
democracy" or in the United States the talismanic power of
the term "grassroots" as a term of high praise and a badge
of authenticity. In the US, civic education has been a kind of
moral rally to encourage participation in public life. But what
kinds of participation are legitimate in a democracy? "Power
to the people" was a slogan of the 1960s, appropriate enough
for a student movement, but juvenile as a political theory.
"Power to the people" should be recognized by now as a
horrifying slogan – not because this people or that people is
bad but that this people and that people, without being checked,
may favor the present over the future, follow passion over
reason, and may be inclined to leave minorities today and
future generations tomorrow unserved and unprotected by
the rule of law.

In US constitutional law, there is a famous footnote ("Footnote Four") to an otherwise obscure case from the 1930s,

The United States v. Carolene Products. In that footnote, Justice Harlan Fiske Stone asks under what conditions the Supreme Court should review the constitutionality of a law with "heightened scrutiny." That is, he took it for granted that the Court should normally give a law duly adopted by the Congress and signed by the president the benefit of the doubt, but he wanted to specify when the Court should consider challenges to the law with more exacting scrutiny. He identifies three conditions:

- when the law violates on its face an express provision of the Constitution;
- when the law concerns the electoral process itself and where the law might be understood to limit the institutional protections for allowing eligible citizens to vote;
- when the law appears to discriminate against "discrete and insular minorities" who, by virtue of their minority status, cannot be expected to win power at the ballot box where they will be inevitably outvoted.

Democracies should be identified not with individuals or the characteristics of individuals, nor even with the legitimacy of electoral systems – but with institutions. These institutions should offer fairness and justice; they should offer and guarantee individual freedoms to pursue life, liberty, and happiness; they should provide for fair and well-protected electoral systems and effective administration and monitoring.

Temporality is in a variety of ways a dimension of governance systems. Where autocracies in their various forms seek streamlined decision-making and efficient outcomes, democracies intentionally require slow, deliberate processes. This has much to do with how to hold governors accountable. The slow pace of democratic processes is often frustrating, but it is essential to making democracy work and to holding governments to account.

Part IV
Afterword

11

Second Thoughts: Schudson on Schudson

This essay appeared in 2017 as a response to nine critical assessments of my writings about journalism and politics in a special issue of *Journalism Studies* dedicated to my work and entitled, "The Unlovable Press: Conversations with Michael Schudson." The occasion of that symposium is described below. This chapter serves as an afterword that may help readers see beneath and behind the other papers in this volume, reaching to the personal and intellectual inclinations and disinclinations that have shaped them.

I am so grateful to Marcel Broersma for proposing my name to the University of Groningen for an honorary degree in 2014. On that special occasion – the 400th anniversary of the university's founding – he went further to organize a conference built around my work. The contributions in this issue of *Journalism Studies* were first presented there.[1]

I am grateful also to Bob Franklin for dedicating many pages of *Journalism Studies* to this symposium. And I am very grateful indeed to the care that my colleagues in both Europe and the United States have taken with my words. That some of these colleagues are former students of mine makes this occasion even more splendid. It is a great gift that several of these papers restate my arguments more eloquently and reformulate them more aptly than I did myself.

I can't take on all the provocative points raised in these papers and, the truth is, I don't need to, since they all speak so well for themselves. But I will take this opportunity to comment on a few issues. One is my relative neglect of technology and economics in understanding the production and significance of journalism – or, to turn that around, to reflect on what might be the costs in my culture-centered approach. Second, can my early work on journalism be understood as an exercise in the sociology of knowledge? Third, what is to be gained, if anything, for journalism studies by my ventures into a broader political history, particularly in *The Good Citizen* (1998) and *The Rise of the Right to Know* (2015)? And finally, what praise or blame should be attached to my style or sensibility, particularly to my "optimism" – if optimism it is?

What's Missing: Is Schudson's Work Too Culture-Centered?

Several of these papers argue that my work omits or underplays the role of economic forces in the development and operation of American journalism (both Rodney Benson and Martin Conboy) and that I have likewise neglected the powerful role of technology in media history (Christoph Raetzsch).

This criticism is fair – up to a point. In the 1970s the academic left was attached to a Marxist vocabulary for understanding society. This meant a strong inclination to see economics (and sometimes technology) as society's base, the fundamental explanation of its "superstructural" political, sociological, and cultural features. This emphasis got at a piece of the truth and then blew it up into a balloon of misunderstanding. Later, the academic left turned to cultural analysis and an emphasis on "texts" (sometimes to the exclusion of an empirical look at society), but a view that the economy is the basis of everything else lingered, and not just on the left.

At least in the US, "it's the economy, stupid" is a reflex that pushes us to ignore other forces in society and also blinds us to the ways commercialism is itself progressive. Progressive? Yes, indeed. Where, in the writings of Habermas about the great opening of the public sphere in the eighteenth century, is much made of the fact that commerce was the handmaiden of the public sphere? The public sphere grew up in the nursery of the coffee house and the pub (both commercial operations) and the newspaper – a business venture even before it was a political project. It is not easy to conceive how a public sphere could have endured for very long without commercial sustenance. Even where public media are so much stronger than in the United States, as they are in parts of Europe, they have sometimes been prodded to boldness by the introduction of commercial competition, learning from their rivals to hold governments and parties accountable (as in the case of the BBC's new willingness, beginning in the mid-1950s, to cover domestic political conflict and controversy).

Growing up, I saw a human face of small-time capitalism. One of my grandfathers was a fabric salesman and the other the owner of a handful of men's clothing stores. My father ran a small sporting goods and sports (bowling) apparel business. It employed about 40 people at its height. When I worked for my Dad in the stock room and the office summers, I saw that he was a kind of uncredentialed social worker. His employees were employees – he hired them, he fired them. I doubt that he paid them great wages. (He paid me minimum wage, which is about what I was worth.) But he knew his employees as human beings. They had family problems. They had troublesome teenagers. They had spouses with drinking problems. They were sometimes late to work. He listened to them. He worried about them. He helped them outside the contractual bounds of the employer–employee relationship. (On occasion, he hired *their* children for summer jobs, too, not just his own.)

Capitalism is also the corner supermarket a few blocks from me in New York, where the cashiers know and treat with patience and kindness several lonely, elderly men in the neighborhood who stop in for a little conversation. Capitalism built the finest examples of journalism the United States has produced, whether the Sulzberger family at the *New York Times* or the Graham family at the *Washington Post* or the Chandlers at the *Los Angeles Times*.

I am not blind to the ways marketplace incentives have pushed the fossil fuel industry to impede environmentalism or to the ways the tobacco industry knowingly contributed to lung cancer – and I have made modest contributions to the literature on the tobacco companies.[2] The marketplace is powerful. Economic incentives and business competition are powerful factors in human affairs, but I think that economics is rarely the only or the first thing to consider in understanding complex human actions. It is a mistake to see what has become of journalism in the past half century as primarily the story of "market failure." The first big thing that happened, beginning in the late 1960s, was a huge growth and improvement in the critical quality of news. To say that "investigative reporting, especially at the local level, is declining" (as Rodney Benson does, citing the admirable work of sociologist Paul Starr) seems to me incomplete. One has to say first that it is declining (to the extent that it is) from a height reached only in the late 1960s and the 1970s. When Benson adds that "the amount of critical business reporting relative to the power wielded by business is still woefully inadequate," I agree, but with the same sort of qualification. When was business reporting not inadequate (or where? has it been strong in Britain or France or Germany or Finland)? Journalist Robert Samuelson joined the *Washington Post* business staff in 1969 – bringing the grand total of writers on the business desk to seven. There would be more than 80 by 2002. In 1969, Samuelson later recalled, "critical reporting was often conspicuous by its absence."[3] Business reporting today, despite the weak market for journalism, is stronger than at any point in American history before the 1970s. A more investigative, analytical, contextual, and critical reporting since 1970 began and gained traction with economic permission (many news organizations were prosperous) but without economic or technological impetus.

Christoph Raetzsch focuses on how my work underestimates the importance of technology. Yes, I am usually making a case against technological determinism. I have been doing so from *Discovering the News* (1978) on, and I will likely continue in the same vein – not because technology is unimportant but because far too regularly social science and, even more, popular commentary finds it to be all that matters. Raetzsch finds my neglect of technology particularly regrettable at the present moment when new technology not only changes institutions of journalism, but alters the dynamics of the formation of publics. He calls for examining "how publics are forming beyond its [journalism's] institutional framework." He makes this point well. He is right to urge us to study publics where they are arising and to relax the assumption that the theater of public-ness lives only when people respond to "news" produced by the professionalized institutions that have dominated for a century. At the same time, we should recognize that these old-line news organizations, now outpaced by upstart organizations and networks in the *distribution* of news, still dominate the *gathering* and *producing* of original reports on contemporary affairs. They remain a central agency of public-formation. Will this be true in another 20 years? I do not know the future.

Is Schudson Doing The Sociology of Knowledge?

Christoph Raetzsch writes that I remain "at heart...a sociologist" and I agree. Chris Anderson portrays me specifically as a sociologist of knowledge. That is perhaps a more surprising claim, but I think it is also right. In graduate school and ever since I have been drawn to the sociology of knowledge. Perhaps it was this long acquaintance that made me puzzled by science and technology studies (STS) that has drawn the enthusiasm of so many of my finest students. Fred Turner tried to explain STS to me when he was a graduate student of mine at UCSD. What was there in STS, I wondered, that I had not read in Peter Berger and Thomas Luckmann's *Social Construction of Reality* (1966) around 1970? A greater emphasis on technology, yes. A greater interest in the materiality of tools and processes and in the microprocesses of "laboratory life." But the heart of the matter – that what we count as "knowledge" is a product of social relations, social processes, and social institutions – that much was all there in Berger and Luckmann.

When I was in graduate school in the 1970s, what was not to be found in the sociology of knowledge as far as I knew (but I knew very little of the sociology of science) was concrete, empirical study of knowledge formation. The sociology of knowledge seemed a strictly theoretical enterprise and I was drawn more to the empirical and the historical. I conceived my dissertation as a study in the sociology of professions, with case studies of journalism and law. And it may well be, as Anderson suggests, that *Discovering the News* would have demonstrated its intellectual location better if I had retained more of the "law" part of the dissertation at least in my discussion of the cultural spirit of the post-World War I era.

Why the narrowing from dissertation to book? Editor Martin Kessler at Basic Books wanted the simpler story of journalism. So did Morris Janowitz, my senior colleague at the University of Chicago and one of the very few sociologists ever to write a book about journalism. They felt what I had to say about journalism was fresh, original – and understandable. "Legal theory" was abstruse. And while I had spent a year sitting in on courses at Harvard Law School, I did not feel myself as securely anchored in law as in journalism.

I agree with Anderson that my work fits into the sociology of knowledge. I think the sociology of knowledge is inherently radical or destabilizing. None of us really likes to believe that the truths we depend on and might even stake our lives on, are historically contingent. But that's how it is. And scientific truths, as Thomas Kuhn told us, following physicist Max Planck, are no exception. When a new theory or "paradigm" replaces an old one, it is not that it won a carefully undertaken evidence-based argument with the old paradigm; it is, as Planck said, that the scientists committed to the old paradigm died off. Science advances, he is supposed to have said, one funeral at a time. This is unduly cynical, in my estimation, but it gets at the heart of the matter.

Brian McNair also focuses on *Discovering the News* (1978) and offers a fine analysis of the book. I very much agree with him that objectivity is as, or more, important than ever today. I differ with him on two points. He writes of a crisis of objectivity in US journalism in the 1990s/2000s highlighted by Stephen Glass's fraud at *The New Republic* and Jayson Blair's at the *New York Times*. But "crisis"? I may misremember, but my recollection is that there was little hesitation about what to do with Glass and Blair – "you're fired!" It was not a crisis of objectivity. Objectivity controversies are about controlling bias, not about policing fraud. The Glass and Blair incidents offered occasions of public theater that reasserted the devotion of news organizations to the pursuit of truth.

The other point is that McNair writes that in the years since the publications of the Glasgow University Media Group in the UK and *Discovering the News* in the US (and on the American side the contemporaneous works of Herbert Gans, Todd Gitlin, Gaye Tuchman, and several others), news organizations have helped readers "peer behind the scenes of the finished product." But has that really happened? McNair sees it at the BBC, and says that generally "news organisations have provided their users/audiences with various tools in which to peer behind the scenes of the finished news product and observe or even participate in the production process." But I do not think the very occasional moments of crowd-sourcing and occasional sidebars on "how I got that story" do very much to give audiences genuine insight into the newsroom process.

Erik Neveu usefully revisits the distinction in *Discovering the News* between "information" journalism and "story" journalism. I agree completely with his criticism that it is inadequate. I knew that at the time. I never much liked my "information/story" distinction. It arose, for me, in the first place because I had been led to believe by the denunciations of "yellow journalism" among historians of US journalism that I would find in Joseph Pulitzer's *World* little but sensationalism. But when I was browsing through the brittle and crumbling pages of *The New York World*, I found a newspaper full of serious news, often colorful news, to be sure, but so far as I could judge (and I simply did not know enough US history in general or New York City history in particular to be a competent judge) this was in fact not the despicable, pandering newspaper I had been led to expect, but a lively effort at news-gathering. Still, the *New York Times* at the same moment (the late 1890s, particularly 1898 and the Spanish-American War) demonstrated a more constrained, gray sobriety. I was not ready to declare one model superior to the other, but they were certainly different. How to name the difference? "Information" versus "story" never seemed to me satisfying, but it was the best idea that came to mind and someone else would have to do better some day.

I think now that there are many more categories of news than "information" and "story" can possibly comprehend, or "hard news" and "feature" or any other pair of terms. The notion of "contextual journalism" that Katherine Fink and I developed in the 2014 paper Neveu refers to is an important additional category.[4] So are the categories Rodney Benson calls attention to in his French–US comparison – the comparative crossnational dimension of news analysis shows the ways that different professional journalisms have developed differently in different nations.[5] Charles Briggs and Daniel Hallin's book on health news (in the US press) shows that there are sharp differences today even in a single news product, different routines and genre markers across different subject areas.[6] We could perhaps find ourselves juggling several dozen story "types" in news analysis or in the norms that guide the coverage of, say, sports ("write from the viewpoint of the home team"), politics ("provide contextual analysis but do not take sides in a partisan battle"), medicine ("defer, normally, to medical authority") – no set of types will have the capacity to map the field of journalism when blends and hybrids seep in everywhere, now more than ever, and will defeat the best typological scheme of the critic.

So is *Discovering the News* an exercise in the sociology of knowledge? I think that's a valuable way to see it – and a good way to categorize several of my later essays, most of all "The Politics of Narrative Form" and "Question Authority: A History of the News Interview," both collected in *The Power of News* (1995).

Did Schudson Move From Being a Sociologist to Being a Political Historian?

My first major in college was political science. I switched to sociology-anthropology (then and still today combined in a single department at Swarthmore College), but I never lost my interest in politics. And I have always loved history. But in college, quite naively, I thought historians had nothing to teach me that I could not pick up on my own by reading some books, while I imagined the social sciences all had recondite concepts and methods that I could learn only in a classroom.

In any event, I have moved into rethinking political culture and political history. Lucas Graves offers a brilliant, subtle condensation of my arguments in *The Good Citizen* and *The Rise of the Right to Know*. I am very pleased to see his account in *Journalism Studies* for this awkward reason: it is both my pleasure and my pain that *Discovering the News*, my first book, is my best known. I think *The Good Citizen* is probably my best book, of broadest compass and offering the sharpest critique of conventional thinking of any of my works. It rejects the model of "the informed citizen" as the only or best model of what democracies require of their citizens. This model governs the self-understanding of American journalists, teachers of high school history, and American public discourse generally, and it is routinely thought to have been what the American founders prized but that is not actually so. What counts as a "good citizen" has changed over the course of 200 years. Like *Discovering the News*, *The Good Citizen* historicizes a value, a norm, an ideal – objectivity in the first case, "being informed" as the chief feature of good citizenship in the second (and, later, "transparency" in *The Rise of the Right to Know*). Knowing the history of political culture helps us understand journalism history, too. Progressive Era efforts to criticize the corruption of parties and partisanship, to nominate candidates through popular primaries rather than smoke-filled rooms; to seek ways for citizens to vote directly on legislation (in propositions and referenda), particularly in states where organized parties were relatively weak – all of this stressed that citizens should become informed rather than that they should be loyal followers of particular parties. This helped open the doors to newspapers less closely identified with parties.

So I am very pleased to see attention to my more recent works in these pages of *Journalism Studies*, notably in the essays of Lucas Graves, Rasmus Kleis Nielsen, and Silvio Waisbord. I agree with the latter that some of my work contributes to much beyond "journalism studies."

Waisbord is sympathetic when I endorse Walter Lippmann's view that democracies depend on the expertise of experts. What I also learn from Lippmann is that his praise of experts is not itself elitist, however elitist his style and taste may have been. That is, he does not think that ordinary people should cede authority to experts because they have less intelligence or fewer years of education or insufficient cultural cultivation to follow and contribute to the intricacies of government. Instead, Lippmann argues that we all fall short in similar ways. None of us is in a strong position to advise government.

The multiple tasks of contemporary government are more than any of us can absorb, including members of Congress who are devoting full-time attention to the job of governing. There's no shame in this. We all have limited cognitive capacities. This includes the Congress; as Lippmann observed in 1922, "the cleverest and most industrious representative cannot hope to understand a fraction of the bills on which he votes. The best he can do is to specialize on a few bills, and take somebody's word about the rest."[7] Moreover, what Lippmann hails in government experts is not their brains or their cultivation, but their independence, their commitment to what their best analysis of the facts commands, not what the president or secretary or Congress would wish. And his case in point is the British foreign service, where, he writes, "the divorce between the assembling of knowledge and the control of policy is most perfect." The virtue of the expert in democracy depends on "not caring, in his expert self, what decision is made."[8]

On Optimism – I Stick With It

Several of the contributors have some doubts about my apparently optimistic tone. Rasmus Kleis Nielsen finds my list of seven things journalism can do for democracy somewhere beyond optimistic – perhaps utopian (I will come back to this). Martin Conboy wonders why I fail to recognize that "journalism in its current form may no longer have the ability to contribute to the democratic project." Looking around us today, Conboy sees that "the very democratic and commercial strengths that appeared to guarantee the triumph of journalism have been swept away." In other words, Professor Schudson, isn't it time to throw optimism overboard?

That would be premature. Look at what's taking place today at the *New York Times*, the *Guardian*, the BBC, the *Washington Post*, ProPublica, the Center for Investigative Journalism, the International Consortium of Investigative Journalists, the Investigative Reporting Workshop, the Center for Public Integrity, the Investigative News Network and its roughly 100 nonprofit member organizations. Small start-ups with no more than half a dozen journalists have demonstrated journalistic prowess and won coveted national prizes, including the Pulitzer Prize. A satisfactory business model? No, not that I can see. At the same time, in a country with limited state support for the arts, modern dance and experimental music and avant-garde theater and poetry and classical music have never had a business model, either. They survive, like most of the journalistic start-ups, on the philanthropy of individuals and foundations. The nonprofitable arts in America have endured and nonprofitable journalism might muddle along the same way.

But then Waisbord adds a related objection to my optimism: if I am right or mostly right that democracy is a better form of government as it has evolved into a monitory democracy with a strong civil society, more watchdog journalism, more critical and skeptical citizens, more comprehensive recognition of and protection of the rights of minorities, and stronger protection of individual rights in general, how is it that some things have gone so badly wrong? Specifically, why is income inequality growing? Does monitorial democracy speak, just as representative, legislature-centered democracy before it, with an upper-class accent?

Yes, it does. But I am less inclined to say that monitory democracy is "better" than election-and-legislature-centered democracy than to say it is better for a democracy with a strong administrative state where the governmental center of gravity has shifted from legislature to executive. And the time is way past due for scholars of journalism to read John Keane's *The Life and Death of Democracy* (2009) or Pierre Rosanvallon's *Counter-Democracy* (2006) for stunning and, to my mind, convincing accounts of why we need to rethink our now surprisingly antiquated concepts of democracy and democratic citizenship.

I agree with almost everything Rasmus Kleis Nielsen writes here. I want to comment only on the point where he distances himself from six-sevenths of what I argue "journalism can do for democracy" in an essay in *Why Democracies Need an Unlovable Press* (2008). My list arose not from the intellectual's study but from the breakfast table, reading newspapers. And I find the *New York Times* (my most regular newspaper fare) takes on the first six of the seven services fairly often. These are: providing information, advocacy, investigating, analyzing, offering a public forum, publicizing how representative democracy works, and conveying social empathy by describing the lives of individuals and communities we may not know. (A perfect example appeared in *The Times* this morning – April 17, 2017 – in a front-page story about a Girl Scout troop made up entirely of homeless girls in a public shelter in New York City.) The only persistent failure, in my view, is that *The Times* is trapped (like most of the rest of us) in the election-centered, "informed citizen"-dominated model of democracy that does not offer readers much illumination about how contemporary democracies operate – the growing role of the administrative state; the growing monitorial and auditing institutions both inside and outside government that seek to hold that administrative state responsible to the Congress and the public; the growing capacity of interest groups and public interest groups to seek political objectives through litigation; and the changing role of citizens when they can exercise their political interests routinely 365 days a year rather than once every couple of years at the voting booth, as the American founders expected. But as for the other six democratic functions, I am not asking news organizations to take on tasks they do not already perform, sometimes breathtakingly well. I am only asking that news organizations recognize each of these functions they have assumed as aiding democracy – not saving democracy, not saving democracy from itself, not guaranteeing utopia, but making significant contributions.

Others also take on some of these functions. Take the investigative function. There is investigative work in the legal process that is crucial to democracy. The investigative portfolio is also shared by inspectors-general and other auditing and investigating services inside the government itself. The fox guarding the henhouse? That's not the weight of the evidence so far. In a civil service that is operating properly, corruption, overreaching, and mismanagement can be patrolled by internal services. Democracy cannot and should not rely exclusively on journalism for investigative reporting, but journalists have well-practiced skills that few prosecutors or inspectors can match – they know how to tell a story and they know how to speak engagingly to a general public.

Nielsen worries that I urge upon journalism far more than it can possibly handle. It would be enough, he believes, if journalism just did a good job of providing information to help citizens navigate their political world. Having worked with journalists regularly, he wants to send a message to academics that there are many, many admirable reporters, photographers, and editors who work bravely and brilliantly to bring us information – let's not burden them with half a dozen other things, too!

I, too, admire journalists. We should not ask them to solve all the world's problems. They never have. They never will. But am I nonetheless too much an optimist? Well, I can't answer that "yes" or "no." I do think that a teacher, any teacher, has an obligation to be optimistic and to believe that a next generation can accomplish great things, greater than we can yet even imagine.

On the other hand, I grew up in the shadow of the Holocaust, in the era of nuclear weapons, in a late adulthood of genocidal conflicts on several continents, in a world of international terrorism that has convulsed the planet, and at a time when many powerful "hear no evil, see no evil" monkeys in the United States ignore potentially catastrophic global warming. Nothing here breeds optimism. "Illiberal democracy" gains ground around the world, and the United States is not exempt. I think most people most of the time do not know or care much about large political issues and, when they do, they are more likely to be inspired by fear than by hope.

If majority rule is the whole of democracy, I am not a democrat. What I admire and cherish is *liberal* democracy – that is, democracy committed to operating by the rule of law, democracy in which protection of minorities is carefully and constitutionally provided, democracy where institutional mechanisms make decision-making work slowly, with multiple chances for public notice and public hearing, amendment, appeal, second thoughts, and opportunities for different groups with different interests to contribute to decisions.

And I worry about what academia, as well as journalism, contributes to democracy. I think it has become too much of a reflex for scholars to criticize. Of course, critique *is* what we do! You cannot publish an academic article in a refereed journal if you have read the relevant literature and think it is all just great! If you can't find fault with it, why should we read something new on the subject?

But if all we do is criticize, why believe us? I heard it said of one scholar that he really had only two lectures to present, whatever the specific topic: "Things are really bad" and "Things are getting worse." We can do better than that. I aspire to an optimism of spirit, but only paired with a realism of assessment.

Notes

Introduction

1 Daniel C. Hallin, "The Passing of the 'High Modernism' of American Journalism," in Hallin, *We Keep America On Top of the World* (New York: Routledge, 1994), pp. 170–180, at p. 171.

2 An early complaint about media coverage of Sanders came from Steve Hendricks, "Bernie Sanders Can't Win: Why the Press Loves to Hate Underdogs," *Columbia Journalism Review*, May 21, 2015; at: www.cjr.org.

3 Margaret Canovan, "Trust the People! Populism and the Two Faces of Democracy," *Political Studies* 47 (1999): 2–16, at p. 14.

4 Bernard Berelson, "What Missing the Newspaper Means," in Paul F. Lazarsfeld and Frank N. Stanton, eds., *Communications Research 1948–1949* (New York: Harper & Brothers, 1949), pp. 111–129.

5 Fareed Zakaria, "The Rise of Illiberal Democracy," *Foreign Affairs*, November/December 1997.

6 Walter Lippmann, *Public Opinion* (New York: Free Press, 1997 [1922]), p. 229.

7 Thomas Patterson, *Out of Order* (New York: Alfred A. Knopf, 1993), p. 20.

8 Leonard Downie, Jr., and Robert G. Kaiser, *The News About the News* (New York: Alfred A. Knopf, 2002), pp. 7–8, 108.

9 Sharon LaFraniere and Nicholas Fandos, "Trump Jr. Won't Provide Details of a Call with His Father," *New York Times*, December 7, 2017, p. A18.

10 For an account of the Flynn case, including President Trump's initial attack on the *Washington Post*'s reporting, see *Washington Post* executive editor Martin Baron's Reuters Memorial Lecture, University of Oxford, February 16, 2018. At https://www.washingtonpost.com/pr/wp/2018/02/19/washington-post-executive-editor-martin-baron-delivers-reuters-memorial-lecture-at-the-university-of-oxford/.

Anthony Scaramucci's fall began when he made a phone call to *New Yorker* reporter Ryan Lizza and, not fully aware or not really caring that this was all on-the-record and that Lizza was recording the entire interview, made scandalous accusations about other top White House staff in vulgarity-laden language. See Ryan Lizza's "Scaramucci Called Me to Unload," *New Yorker*, July 27, 2017. At https://www.newyorker.com/news/ryan-lizza/anthony-scaramucci-called-me-to-unload-about-white-house-leakers-reince-priebus-and-steve-bannon.

For Tom Price, see the first of a series of stories by Dan Diamond and Rachana Pradhan in *Politico*: "Price's Private-Jet Travel Breaks Precedent." See also an account by Diamond and Pradhan of how they did the research on the series that forced Price to resign his position. At https://www.politico.com/magazine/story/2017/10/04/how-we-found-tom-prices-private-jets-215680.

For Brenda Fitzgerald, see Sheila Kaplan, "Dr. Brenda Fitzgerald, CDC Director, Resigns Over Tobacco and Other Investments," *New York Times*, January 31, 2018, crediting *Politico* for its original reporting. The original story was by Sarah Karlin-Smith and Brianna Ehley, "Trump's Top Health Official Traded Tobacco Stock While Leading Anti-Smoking Efforts," *Politico*, January 30, 2018. At https://www.politico.com/story/2018/01/30/cdc-director-tobacco-stocks-after-appointment-316245.

For Rob Porter, see DailyMail.com February 12, 2018, with its interviews with Colbie Holderness, Porter's first ex-wife, and Jennifer Willoughby, his second ex-wife. At http://www.dailymail.co.uk/news/article-5359731/Ex-wife-Rob-Porter-Trumps-secretary-tells-marriage.html. Also see media columnist Margaret Sullivan's commentary in the *Washington Post*, February 12, 2018: "Will Truth Win Out? Rob Porter's Departure Holds a Key to Effective Journalism in the Trump Era."

11 Lippmann, *Public Opinion*, p. 230.

12 Peter Parisi, "Astonishment and Understanding: On the Problem of Explanation in Journalism," *New Jersey Journal of Communication* 7 (1999), p. 7.

13 Walter Lippmann, *Liberty and the News* (Princeton: Princeton University Press, 2008 [1920]), pp. 58–59. The title essay, "Liberty

and the News," from which I have quoted here, first appeared in *The Atlantic Magazine*, December 1919, pp. 779–786.

Chapter 1   14 or 15 Generations: News as a Cultural Form and Journalism as a Historical Formation

1 Bill Kovach and Tom Rosenstiel, *The Elements of Journalism* (New York: Three Rivers Press, 2007), p. 12.
2 Kovach and Rosenstiel, *Elements of Journalism*, p. 12.
3 Kovach and Rosenstiel, *Elements of Journalism*, p. 15, quoting Mitchell Stephens, *A History of News* (Fort Worth, TX: Harcourt Brace College Publishers, 1996), p. 27.
4 Charles E. Clark and Charles Wetherell, "The Measure of Maturity: The Pennsylvania Gazette, 1728–1765," *William and Mary Quarterly* 46, no. 2 (April 1989): 279–303.
5 Eugen Weber, *Peasants Into Frenchmen* (Stanford, CA: Stanford University Press, 1976), pp. 468–469.
6 Robin Jeffrey, *India's Newspaper Revolution: Capitalism, Politics and the Indian Language Press*, 3rd ed. (New Delhi: Oxford University Press, 2009), p. 87, quoting Swaminath Natarajan, *History of the Press in India* (New York: Asia Pub. House, 1962), p. 323.
7 Charles Peters, *Five Days in Philadelphia: The Amazing "We Want Willkie!" Convention of 1940 and How It Freed FDR to Save the Western World* (New York: Public Affairs, 2005).
8 Kovach and Rosenstiel, *Elements of Journalism*, p. 15.
9 Claude Lévi-Strauss, *Tristes Tropiques* (New York: Atheneum, 1969), p. 292.
10 Marcel Broersma writes of sharp changes in the Dutch press after 1945 as the Dutch newspaper came to accept "Anglo-American conventions" of news presentation. And what were these conventions? They were that journalists now focused on "news value" in which they did not offer a long-winded report that noted chronologically the course of a meeting or other event but instead offered a "short, matter-of-fact, appetizing report" in which the journalist identified the most important information. In the key sentence in Broersma's essay, he observes, "Journalists (after 1945) were no longer expected merely to record happenings but to extract the news from an event." See Marcel Broersma, "Visual Strategies, Dutch Newspaper Design between Text and Image, 1900–2000," in Broersma, ed., *Form and Style in Journalism: European Newspapers and the Representation of News, 1880–2005* (Leuven: Peeters, 2007), pp. 177–198.

On the UK Donald Matheson argues that a distinctive "news discourse" in Britain emerged in the years 1880–1930. For Matheson, the multitude of eclectic styles in the Victorian newspaper all became subsumed in a single news discourse; and news became less a collection of raw information and more "a form of knowledge in itself," much as Broersma suggests for the Netherlands half a century later. I am oversimplifying subtle arguments in both papers, but I think the simplification is true to their argument – that what you and I recognize intuitively as journalism is, in the United States, just over a century old, in Britain just under a century old, and in the Netherlands about 60 years old. See Donald Matheson, "The Birth of News Discourse: Changes in News Language in British Newspapers, 1880–1930," *Media, Culture, and Society* 22 (2000): 557–573.

11 Isaiah Berlin, "The Counter-Enlightenment," in Berlin, *Against the Current: Essays in the History of Ideas* (New York: Viking Press, 1980), p. 20.

12 Berlin, "The Counter-Enlightenment," p. 1.

13 This is a topic for another essay, not this one, but I have made the case for it directly or indirectly in *The Good Citizen: A History of American Civic Life* (New York: Free Press, 1998) and *The Sociology of News* (New York: W. W. Norton, 2011).

14 Jürgen Habermas, *The Structural Transformation of the Public Sphere: An Inquiry into a Category of Bourgeois Society* (Cambridge, MA: MIT Press, 1989), p. 401.

15 Stuart Firestein, *Ignorance: How It Drives Science* (New York: Oxford University Press, 2012), p. 166.

Chapter 2   Walter Lippmann's Ghost: An Interview

1 Walter Lippmann, *Public Opinion* (New York: Free Press, 1997 [1922]); *Liberty and the News* (Princeton: Princeton University Press, 2008 [1920]).

2 Katherine Fink and Michael Schudson, "The Rise of Contextual Reporting, 1950s–2000s," *Journalism: Theory, Practice, Criticism* 15, no. 1 (January 2014): 3–20.

3 Lippmann, *Liberty and the News*, pp. 73–4.

4 Lippmann, *Liberty and the News*, p. 81.

5 Lippmann, *Liberty and the News*, p. 81.

6 John Keane, *The Life and Death of Democracy* (New York: Simon & Schuster, 2009), p. 817.

7 Richard Posner, "The Rise and Fall of Administrative Law," *Chicago-Kent Law Review*, 72 (1996): 953–963, at p. 954.

8 Council of the Inspectors General on Integrity and Efficiency. At https://www.ignet.gov/.

9 Michael Schudson, *The Rise of the Right to Know: Politics and the Culture of Transparency 1945–1975* (Cambridge, MA: Harvard University Press, 2015).

10 Michael Schudson, "The 'Lippmann–Dewey Debate' and the Invention of Walter Lippmann as an Anti-Democrat 1985–1996," *International Journal of Communication* 2, (2008): 1031-1042. Sue Curry Jansen, *Walter Lippmann: A Critical Introduction to Media and Communication Theory* (New York: Peter Lang, 2012).

11 Lippman, *Public Opinion*, p. 229.

Chapter 3   Is Journalism a Profession? Objectivity 1.0, Objectivity 2.0, and Beyond

1 Robert J. Samuelson, "Snob Journalism," *Washington Post*, April 23, 2003.

2 Barbie Zelizer makes the argument that it has been a conceptual mistake to frame journalism within a sociology of professions; it just isn't a profession, in her view, but an "interpretive community," and we will misunderstand it if we try to measure it against familiar signs of "profession." See her "Journalists as Interpretive Communities," *Critical Studies in Mass Communication* 10 (September 1993): 219–137 included under the title of "A Return to Journalists as Interpretive Communities," in Zelizer, *What Journalism Could Be* (Cambridge, UK: Polity, 2017), pp. 175–192. I like her notion of "interpretive community," but I also think there is something to be said for seeing journalism as a kind of profession. Journalism has attained a broad cultural centrality and cultural authority, something very few interpretive communities achieve, and many do not even aspire to – non-proselytizing religious groups, for example.

3 Jean K. Chalaby, "Journalism as an Anglo-American Invention: A Comparison of the Development of French and Anglo-American Journalism, 1830s–1920s," *European Journal of Communication* 11, no. 3 (1996): 303–326.

4 William T. Stead, *The Americanization of the World* (New York: Garland, 1972 [1902]), p. 111.

5 Cited in Donald A. Ritchie, *Press Gallery: Congress and the Washington Correspondents* (Cambridge, MA: Harvard University Press, 1991), pp. 82–83.

6 *New York World*, January 29, 1871. For more on the American origins of interviewing, see Michael Schudson, "Question Authority: A History of the News Interview," *Media, Culture & Society* 16 (October 1994); repr. in Schudson, *The Power of News* (Cambridge, MA: Harvard University Press, 1995), pp. 72–93.

7 See Michael Schudson, "The Politics of Narrative Form" in Schudson, *The Power of News*, pp. 53–71.

8 Donald Matheson, "The Birth of News Discourse: Changes in News Language in British Newspapers, 1880–1930," *Media, Culture & Society* 22 (2000): 557-573, at p. 557.

9 Matheson, "The Birth of News Discourse," p. 562.

10 Matheson, "The Birth of News Discourse," p. 563.

11 On the nascent self-consciousness of reporters as an occupational group in the late nineteenth century, see Michael Schudson, *Discovering the News: A Social History of American Newspapers* (New York: Basic Books, 1978).

12 See Marcel Broersma, "Visual Strategies: Dutch Newspaper Design Between Text and Image 1900-2000," in Marcel Broersma, ed., *Form and Style in Journalism* (Leuven: Peeters, 2007), pp. 177–197.

13 Asa Briggs, *The History of Broadcasting in the United Kingdom*, vol 4: *Sound and Vision* (Oxford: Oxford University Press, 1979), pp. 605–612.

14 Gaye Tuchman "Objectivity as Strategic Ritual: An Examination of Newsmen's Notions of Objectivity," *American Journal of Sociology* 77 (January 1972): 660–679.

15 John Nerone, "The Historical Roots of the Normative Model of Journalism," *Journalism* 14, no. 4 (2013): 446–458, at p. 447.

16 Zelizer, *What Journalism Could Be*, pp. 175–182.

17 Daniel C. Hallin, *We Keep America on Top of the World* (New York: Routledge, 1994).

18 On Washington, see Michael Schudson, *The Good Citizen: A History of American Civic Life* (New York: Free Press, 1998), p. 70; on Jefferson, see Leonard W. Levy, *Freedom of the Press from Zenger to Jefferson* (Durham, NC: Carolina Academic Press, 1996 [1966]), pp. 362–371; and on Theodore Roosevelt's "muckraker" speech, see Doris Kearns Goodwin, *The Bully Pulpit* (New York: Simon & Schuster, 2013), pp. 467–496.

19 According to Nixon's speech writer William Safire, "In the Nixon White House, the press became 'the media,' because the word had a manipulative, Madison Avenue, all-encompassing connotation, and the press hated it." See William Safire, *Before the Fall: An Inside View of the Pre-Watergate White House* (New York: Da Capo Press, 1975), p. 351.

20 David Greenberg, *A History of Spin* (New York: W. W. Norton, 2016).

21 Donald R. Matthews, *US Senators and Their World* (New York: Vintage Books, 1960), p. 207.

22 Matthews, *US Senators and Their World*, p. 214.

23 For examples, see Michael Schudson, "Persistence of Vision: Partisan Journalism in the Mainstream Press," in Carl F. Kaestle and Janice A. Radway, eds., *A History of the Book in America*, vol. 4: *Print in Motion* (Chapel Hill, NC: University of North Carolina Press, 2009), pp. 140–150.

24 Julian E. Zelizer, "Without Restraint: Scandal and Politics in America," in M. C. Carnes, ed., *The Columbia History of Post-World War II America* (New York: Columbia University Press 2007), p. 230.

25 For a fuller account, see Michael Schudson, *The Rise of the Right to Know: Politics and the Culture of Transparency 1945–1975* (Cambridge, MA: Harvard University Press, 2015).

26 Zelizer, "Without Restraint," p. 236.

27 Kathy R. Forde, "Discovering the Explanatory Report in American Newspapers," *Journalism Practice* 1 (2007): 230.

28 Stephen Hess, "Washington Reporters," *Society* 18, no. 4 (1981): 57.

29 Kevin G. Barnhurst, and Diana Mutz, "American Journalism and the Decline in Event-Centered Reporting," *Journal of Communication* 47, no. 4 (1997): 27–52, at p. 32; see also Kevin G. Barnhurst "The Great American Newspaper," *The American Scholar* (Winter 1991): 110. Barnhurst's research is consistent with Stepp's findings. Stepp found a large reduction between 1964 and 1999 in the number of very short stories (under 6 inches long) in the 10 metropolitan dailies he examined and a substantial increase in very long stories (more than 20 inches). See Carl Sessions Stepp, "Then and Now," *American Journalism Review* 21 (1999): 60–75, at p. 62.

30 Stepp, "Then and Now," p. 65.

31 Stepp, "Then and Now," p. 62.

32 Lucas Graves, unpublished interview with Max Frankel, February 24, 2009, transcript in my possession.

33 Thomas Patterson, *Out of Order* (New York: Knopf, 1993), pp. 82–83.

34 Kevin G. Barnhurst, "The Problem of Modern Time in American Journalism," *KronoScope* 11 (2011): 98–123, at p. 114.

35 Katherine Fink and Michael Schudson, "The Rise of Contextual Reporting, 1950s–2000s," *Journalism: Theory, Practice, Criticism* 15, no. 1 (January 2014): 3–20.

36 Meg Greenfield, *Washington* (New York: Public Affairs, 2001), p. 89.
37 Greenfield, *Washington*, p. 85.
38 See Monika Djerf-Pierre, "Squaring the Circle: Public Service and Commercial News on Swedish Television, 1956–99," *Journalism Studies* 1 (2000): 239–260; Ellis Krauss, "Changing Television News in Japan," *Journal of Asian Studies* 57 (1998): 663–692; Paddy Scannell, "Public Service Broadcasting and Modern Public Life," *Media, Culture & Society* 11 (1989): 135–166; and Silvio Waisbord, "The Narrative of Exposés in South American Journalism," *Gazette* 59 (1997): 189–203.

Chapter 4   The Danger of Independent Journalism

1 Daniel C. Hallin, *The "Uncensored War": The Media and Vietnam* (New York: Oxford University Press, 1986), p. 78.
2 Hallin, *The "Uncensored War"*, p. 70.
3 W. Lance Bennett, "Toward a Theory of Press-State Relations," *Journal of Communication* 40 (1990): 103–125.
4 Eric Darras, "Media Consecration of the Political Order," in Rodney Benson and Erik Neveu, eds., *Bourdieu and the Journalistic Field* (Cambridge, UK: Polity, 2005), pp. 156–173.
5 *Miami Herald Publishing Company v. Tornillo* 418 US 241 (1974), p. 260.
6 Pierre Bourdieu, "The Political Field, the Social Science Field, and the Journalistic Field" in Benson and Neveu, eds., *Bourdieu and the Journalistic Field*, pp. 29–47, at p. 45.
7 On the cult, see the classic study by Stanley Schachter, *When Prophecy Fails* (Minneapolis: University of Minnesota Press, 1956). On science, see Thomas S. Kuhn, *The Structure of Scientific Revolutions* (Chicago, IL: University of Chicago Press, 1962).
8 Eric Klinenberg, "Channeling into the Journalistic Field: Youth Activism and the Media Justice Movement" in Benson and Neveu, eds., *Bourdieu and the Journalistic Field*, pp. 174–192.
9 Janet Steele, "Experts and the Operational Bias of Television News: The Case of the Persian Gulf War," *Journalism and Mass Communication Quarterly* 72 (1995): 799–812.
10 John Zaller, "Elite Leadership of Mass Opinion: New Evidence from the Gulf War," in W. Lance Bennett and David Paletz, eds., *Taken by Storm* (Chicago, IL: University of Chicago Press, 1994), pp. 186–209, esp. pp. 201–202.
11 Herbert J. Gans, *Deciding What's News* (New York: Pantheon, 1979).

Chapter 5 Belgium Invades Germany: Reclaiming Non-Fake News – Imperfect, Professional, and Democratic

1 Hannah Arendt, "Truth and Politics," *The New Yorker*, February 25, 1967, pp. 49–88. (Repr. in Hannah Arendt, *Between Past and Future: Eight Exercises in Political Thought* (New York: Viking, 1968) pp. 227–264).
2 Arendt, "Truth and Politics," p. 50.
3 Arendt, "Truth and Politics," p. 52.
4 Arendt, "Truth and Politics," p. 52.
5 Arendt, "Truth and Politics," pp. 88, 84.
6 Arendt, "Truth and Politics," p. 84.
7 Max Planck, quoted in Thomas S. Kuhn, *The Structure of Scientific Revolutions* (Chicago, IL: University of Chicago Press, 1970 [1962]), p. 150.
8 Michael Patrick Lynch, *The Internet of Us* (New York: Liveright, 2016), p. 23.
9 Lynch, *The Internet of Us*, p. 131.
10 Richard Hofstadter, *The Paranoid Style in American Politics* (New York: Knopf, 1966), pp. 36–38.
11 My contribution is particularly in *Discovering the News: A Social History of American Newspapers* (New York: Basic Books, 1978). Other relevant work includes Richard Kaplan, *Politics and the American Press: The Rise of Objectivity, 1865–1920* (Cambridge, UK: Cambridge University Press, 2002), who rightly does much more than I did to integrate the changing character of late nineteenth-century politics into the story. Borrowing from the important work of Michael McGerr, *The Decline of Popular Politics: The American North, 1865-1928* (New York: Oxford University Press, 1986) on changes in "political style" – changing beliefs and practices concerning how electoral politics should be done – I came to pay greater attention to changing popular attitudes toward politics as a contributing factor to professionalization in *The Good Citizen: A History of American Civic Life* (New York: Free Press, 1998).
12 For an illuminating account of the rise of fact-checking organizations and a detailed account of how they operate, see Lucas Graves, *Deciding What's True: The Rise of Political Fact-Checking in American Journalism* (New York: Columbia University Press, 2016).
13 Both the Lewis and Forster quotations are cited in John Keane, *The Life and Death of Democracy* (New York: Simon & Schuster, 2009), pp. 865, 867, a work to which I am much indebted.

14 "Communicating Science in an Age of Disbelief in Experts," *Bulletin of the American Academy of Arts & Sciences* (Summer 2017): 26–34.

Chapter 6 Journalism in a Journalized Society: Reflections on Raymond Williams and the "Dramatized Society"

1 The lecture is reprinted in Jim McGuigan, ed., *Raymond Williams on Culture & Society* (London: Sage, 2014), pp. 161–172
2 *Raymond Williams on Culture & Society*, p. 161.
3 *Raymond Williams on Culture & Society*, p. 162.
4 *Raymond Williams on Culture & Society*, p. 164.
5 *Raymond Williams on Culture & Society*, p. 164.
6 *Raymond Williams on Culture & Society*, p. 165.
7 Soomin Seo, "Virtual Foreign Bureaus and the New Ecology of International News," PhD dissertation, Columbia University, Program on Communication, 2016.
8 Svennik Hoyer and Horst Pottker, eds., *Diffusion of the News Paradigm 1850–2000* (Goteborg, Sweeden: NORDICOM, 2005).
9 Svennik Hoyer and John Nonseid, "The Half-Hearted Modernisation of Norwegian Journalism 1908-1940," in Hoyer and Pottker, *Diffusion of the News Paradigm*, pp. 123–138, at p. 124
10 Hoyer and Nonseid, "Half-Hearted Modernisation," p. 134.
11 See Andrea Umbricht and Frank Esser, "Changing Political News? Long-Term Trends in American, British, French, Italian, German, and Swiss Print Media Reporting," in Raymond Kuhn and Rasmus Kleis Nielsen, eds., *Political Journalism in a Comparative Perspective* (London: I. B. Tauris, 2014), as well as other essays in the same useful volume.
12 Hoyer and Nonseid, "Half-Hearted Modernisation," p. 135.
13 Marcel Broersma, "Visual Strategies: Dutch Newspaper Design Between Text and Image 1900–2000," in Marcel Broersma, ed., *Form and Style in Journalism. European Newspapers and the Representation of News, 1880-2005* (Leuven: Peeters, 2007), pp. 177–198, at p. 187.
14 Donald Matheson, "The Birth of News Discourse: Changes in News Language in British Newspapers, 1880–1930," *Media, Culture, and Society* 22 (2000): 557–573, at p. 559.
15 Matheson, "The Birth of News Discourse," p. 564.
16 Daniel Hallin, *We Keep America On Top of the World* (New York: Routledge, 1994), p. 170.

17 On the role of American journalism schools in articulating professional norms, see Tim P. Vos, "Homo Journalisticus: Journalism education's role in articulating the objectivity norm," *Journalism: Theory, Practice, and Criticism* 13 (2012): 435–449.

18 Monika Djerf-Pierre and Lennart Weibull, "From Public Educator to Interpreting Ombudsman: Regimes of Political Journalism in Swedish Public Broadcasting," in Jesper Strömbëck, Mark Ørsten, and Toril Aalberg, eds., *Communicating Politics: Political Communication in the Nordic Countries* (Goteborg: Nordicom, 2008), pp. 195–214.

19 Bernard Berelson, "What Missing the Newspaper Means," in Paul F. Lazarsfeld and Frank N. Stanton, eds., *Communications Research 1948–1949* (New York: Harper & Brothers, 1949), pp. 111–129.

20 Daniel Dayan and Elihu Katz, *Media Events: The Live Broadcasting of History* (Cambridge, MA: Harvard University Press, 1992).

21 Raymond Williams, *Television: Technology and Cultural Form* (London: Fontana, 1974); Roger Silverstone, "Preface," in Williams, *Television: Technology and Cultural Form* (Milton Park, UK: Routledge Classics, 2003), pp. viii–ix.

22 David M. Ryfe, *Can Journalism Survive? An Inside Look at American Newsrooms* (Cambridge, UK: Polity, 2012), p. 140.

23 John Koblin, "Netflix Lets Viewers Pick the Plot," *New York Times*, June 21, 2017, p. B1.

24 See Michael Schudson, *Discovering the News: A Social History of American Newspapers* (New York: Basic Books, 1978), pp. 144–154.

25 David Stark, *The Sense of Dissonance* (Princeton, NJ: Princeton University Press, 2009), p. 1.

26 Nicholas A. John, *The Age of Sharing* (Cambridge, UK: Polity, 2017).

27 Fred Turner, *From Counter-Culture to Cyberculture: Steward Brand, the Whole Earth Network, and the Rise of Digital Utopianism* (Chicago, IL: University of Chicago Press, 2006).

Chapter 7   The Crisis in News: Can You Whistle a Happy Tune?

1 Johannes Weber, "Strassburg, 1605: The Origins of the Newspaper in Europe," *German History* 24, no. 3 (2006): 387–412.

2 See, for instance Frank Kermode, "Life and Death of the Novel," *New York Review of Books*, October 28, 1965: "The special fate of the novel, considered as a genre, is to be always dying."

3 See a good discussion of this in Rachel Smolkin, "Cities Without Newspapers," *American Journalism Review* 31, no. 3 (June/July 2009): 16–25.

4 David Carr, "Papers are Down, And Now Out," *New York Times*, August 11, 2014, p. B1.

5 Carr, "Papers are Down, And Now Out," p. B4.

6 I attended the conference and these are Carr's words as I remember them. They may not be exactly what he said, but Carr confirmed with me in an email that this is the gist of what he said. The conference – "The Future of Journalism: Who Will Pay the Messengers?" – took place at Yale Law School, November 13–14, 2009.

7 Clay Shirky, "Last Call: The End of the Printed Newspaper." At https://medium.com/@cshirky/last-call-c682f6471c70.

8 Pew Research Center, *State of the News Media (2014)*. At http://www.pewresearch.org/topics/state-of-the-news-media/2014/.

9 See David A. L. Levy and Rasmus Kleis Nielsen, eds., *The Changing Business of Journalism and Its Implications for Democracy* (Oxford: Reuters Institute for the Study of Journalism, 2010); Raymond Kuhn and Rasmus Kleis Nielsen, eds., *Political Journalism in Transition: Western Europe in a Comparative Perspective* (London: I. B. Tauris, 2014).

10 All the data in this paragraph comes from the Pew Research Center, *State of the News Media (2013)*. At http://www.pewresearch.org/topics/state-of-the-news-media/2013/.

11 Pew Research Center, "Amid Criticism, Support for Media's 'Watchdog' Role Stands Out" (August 8, 2013), p. 13. At http://www.people-press.org/2013/08/08/amid-criticism-support-for-medias-watchdog-role-stands-out/. Based on a survey conducted July 17–21, 2013.

12 Pew Research Center, "America's Shifting Statehouse Press" (July 10, 2014), pp. 6, 11. At http://www.journalism.org/2014/07/10/americas-shifting-statehouse-press/.

13 Carl Sessions Stepp, "The State of the American Newspaper: Then and Now," *American Journalism Review* 21 (1999): 60–75. See also other relevant references in Katherine Fink and Michael Schudson, "The Rise of Contextual Journalism, 1950s–2000s," *Journalism: Theory, Criticism, Practice* 15, no. 1 (January 2014): 3–20.

14 Robert J. Samuelson, "Moving Toward the Mainstream," *Nieman Reports* (June 15, 2002). At www.niemanreports.org/articles/moving-toward-the-mainstream/.

15 John Keane, *The Life and Death of Democracy* (New York: Simon & Schuster, 2009) and Pierre Rosanvallon, *Counter-Democracy* (Cambridge, UK: Cambridge University Press, 2008).

16 Jeremy W. Peters, "Covering 2012, Youths on the Bus," *New York Times*, August 30, 2011; and Wikipedia entry on "Helen Thomas."

17 On the editorial practice of withholding "click" counts from reporters, I rely on Caitlin Petre, *The Traffic Factories*, a Tow Center Report, Tow Center for Digital Journalism, Columbia Journal School. At https://academiccommons.columbia.edu/catalog/ac:kd51c59zxv.

18 David Carr, "Risks Abound as Reporters Play in Traffic," *New York Times*, March 24, 2014, pp. B1, B6.

19 Dean Starkman, "The Hamster Wheel," *Columbia Journalism Review* (September, October, 2010), pp. 24–28, at p. 26.

20 Carr, "Risks Abound," p. B6.

21 Pew Research Center, "America's Shifting Statehouse Press," p. 5, reports the American Society of Newspaper Editors data that there was a 30 percent decline of employees in daily newspaper newsrooms between 2003 and 2012.

22 Pew Research Center, "America's Shifting Statehouse Press."

23 Rodney Benson, "Why Narrative is Not Enough: Immigration and the Genres of Journalism" in Giovanna Dell'Orto and Vicki L. Birchfield, eds., *Reporting at the Southern Borders: Journalism and the Public Debates on Immigration in the US and the EU* (New York: Routledge, 2013); Rodney Benson, *Shaping Immigration News: A French–American Comparison* (New York: Cambridge University Press, 2014).

24 For a round-up of the relevant data, see Fink and Schudson, "The Rise of Contextual Journalism, 1950s–2000s."

25 Quoted in Matthew Powers, "'In Forms That Are Familiar and Yet-to-Be-Invented': American Journalism and the Discourse of Technologically Specific Work," *Journal of Communication Inquiry* 36, no. 1 (2012): 24–43.

26 Alan Rusbridger, "Does Journalism Exist?" This is from a speech delivered in 2010 and published on the website "PaidContent." At http://paidcontent.org/article/419-rusbridger-does-journalism-exist/print/.

27 David Stark, *The Sense of Dissonance* (Princeton, NJ: Princeton University Press, 2009), p. 1.

28 Tim Francisco, Alyssa Lenhoff, and Michael Schudson, "The Classroom as Newsroom: Leveraging University Resources for Public Affairs Reporting," *International Journal of Communication* 6 (2012): 2677–2697.

29 Pam A. Mueller and Daniel M. Oppenheimer, "The Pen Is Mightier Than the Keyboard: Advantages of Longhand Over Laptop Note Taking," *Psychological Science* 25, no. 6 (2014): 1159–1168.

30 Clay Shirky, "Newspapers and Thinking the Unthinkable," March 13, 2009. At http://www.shirky.com/weblog/2009/03newspapers-and-thinking-the-unthinkable/.

31 David Streitfeld, "Doris Dungey, Prescient Finance Blogger, Dies at 47," *New York Times*, November 30, 2008; and an anonymous reader cited in Bill McBride, "In Memoriam: Doris 'Tanta' Dungey," on the blog, *CalculatedRisk*, December 8, 2008. At www.calculatedriskblog.com/2008/12/in-memoriam-doris-tanta-dungey.html.

32 See http://investigativenewsnetwork.org/about/.

Chapter 8   Citizenship – According to "The Simpsons"

1 John F. Reynolds, *Testing Democracy: Electoral Behavior and Progressive Reform in New Jersey, 1880–1920* (Chapel Hill: University of North Carolina Press, 1988), p. 47.

2 James Bryce, *The American Commonwealth*, vol. 2 (Chicago, IL: Charles H. Sergel, 1891), p. 20.

3 Paula Baker, "The Culture of Politics in the Late Nineteenth Century: Community and Political Behavior in Rural New York," *Journal of Social History* 18 (1984): 181.

4 Michael McGerr, *The Decline of Popular Politics* (New York: Oxford University Press, 1986).

5 "The Passing of the Parade," *New York World* 2 (1908): 6.

6 Richard D. Brown, *The Strength of a People: The Idea of an Informed Citizenry in America, 1650–1870* (Chapel Hill: University of North Carolina Press, 1996), p. 44.

7 Brown, *The Strength of a People*, pp. 44, 49.

8 On the politics of self-esteem, see J. L. Nolan, Jr., *The Therapeutic State* (New York: New York University Press, 1998), pp. 152–161.

9 Steve Coll, "Terrorists Turn to the Web as Base of Operations," *Washington Post*, August 7, 2005, p. A-1.

10 "Monitory democracy" is the term John Keane uses in *The Life and Death of Democracy* (New York: Simon & Schuster, 2009). "Counter-democracy" is the term of Pierre Rosanvallon in *Counter-Democracy: Politics in an Age of Distrust*, trans. Arthur Goldhammer (Cambridge, UK: Cambridge University Press, 2006). For "between-election democracy," see Peter Esaiasson and Hanne Marthe Narud, eds., *Between-Election Democracy* (Colchester, UK: ECPR Press, 2013).

Chapter 9   The Multiple Political Roles of American Journalism

1 David E. Pozen, "The Leaky Leviathan: Why the Government Condemns and Condones Unlawful Disclosures of Information," *Harvard Law Review* 127 (2013): 513–635.
2 Cited in David Carr, "Retreading Memories, From a Perch Too Public," *New York Times*, February 9, 2015, p. B1.
3 See Michael Schudson, "Persistence of Vision: Partisan Journalism in the Mainstream Press," in Carl F. Kaestle and Janice A. Radway, eds., *Print in Motion: A History of the Book in America*, vol. 4 (Chapel Hill: University of North Carolina Press, 2009), pp. 140–151.
4 Interview with John Moss, April 13, 1965, in George R. Berdes, *Friendly Adversaries: The Press and Government* (Milwaukee, WI: Center for the Study of the American Press, College of Journalism, Marquette University, 1969), p. 61.
5 George P. Kennedy, "Advocates of Openness: The Freedom of Information Movement," PhD dissertation, University of Missouri, 1978, p. 67. (Kennedy relies here on a 1978 letter to him from Pope.)
6 Address to the Upper Midwest News Executives Conference, Minnesota, Minneapolis, May 3, 1957. John E. Moss Papers, Box 427 Folder 3.
7 Kennedy, "Advocates of Openness," pp. 20–30.
8 A footnote added that school boards barred the public from meetings also in Chicago, Illinois, Columbia, Missouri, Denver, Colorado, Roanoke, Virginia, Providence, Rhode Island, Evansville, Indiana, Flint, Michigan, Baltimore, Maryland, and elsewhere. "Access to Official Information: A Neglected Constitutional Right," *Indiana Law Journal* 27 (1951–2): 209–230.
9 Jacob Scher, "Access to Information: Recent Legal Problems," *Journalism Quarterly* 37 (1960): 41–52.
10 Robert O. Blanchard, "A Watchdog in Decline," *Columbia Journalism Review* (Summer 1966): 17–21, at p. 18.
11 The early history of the Freedom of Information Act is recounted in more detail in Michael Schudson, *The Rise of the Right to Know: Politics and the Culture of Transparency, 1945-1975* (Cambridge, MA: Harvard University Press, 2015).
12 James W. Carey, "A Short History of Journalism for Journalists: A Proposal and Essay," *Harvard International Journal of Press/Politics* 12, no. 1 (2007): 3–16, at p. 13.
13 Susan E. Tifft and Alex S. Jones, *The Trust* (Boston, MA: Little, Brown, 1999) pp. 311–315. See also Max Frankel, *The Times*

of My Life and My Life at The Times (New York: Random House, 1999), p. 209; John F. Stacks, *Scotty: James B. Reston and the Rise and Fall of American Journalism* (Boston, MA: Little, Brown, 2003), p. 192.

14 Bob Woodward, *Veil: The Secret Wars of the CIA, 1981–1987* (New York: Pocket Books, 1988), pp. 516–535.

15 Marcus Brauchli, Third Annual Richard S. Salant Lecture, Joan Shorenstein Center on the Press, Politics and Public Policy, Harvard Kennedy School, Cambridge, MA, October 28, 2010, p. 12. At https://shorensteincenter.org/marcus-brauchli-delivers-2010-richard-s-salant-lecture/.

16 Quoted in Rachel Smolkin, "The Women," *American Journalism Review*, December/January 2004.

17 Cited in Nelson Polsby, *How Congress Evolves* (New York: Oxford University Press, 2004), p. 16.

18 See Norman J. Ornstein and David W. Rohde, "The Strategy of Reform: Recorded Teller Voting in the U.S. House of Representatives," paper prepared for 1974 Midwest Political Science Association convention, Chicago, IL, April 25–27, 1974, p. 1; Steven S. Smith, *Call to Order: Floor Politics in the House and Senate* (Washington, DC: Brookings Institution, 1989), p. 256.

19 Democratic Study Group, "Secrecy in the House of Representatives," June 24, 1970, p. 7. Democratic Study Group (DSG) Papers, Library of Congress, Box 1–4, Folder 7. A fuller account of the passage of the Legislative Reorganization Act and the DSG's role in it can be found in Schudson, *Rise of the Right to Know*.

20 Richard Conlon, interview July 5, 1974. This is a typed transcript of an interview with Conlon in the DSG Papers, Part II, Box 2, Folder 13. There is no indication of who conducted the interview or for what purpose.

21 See the many press clippings in DSG Papers, II-129, Folder 2.

22 DSG Papers, Box I-4, Folder 7, "Special Report: Secrecy in the House of Representatives," June 24, 1970.

23 Thanks to Sam Lebovic and Nicholas Lemann for ideas on this category of political influence.

24 Timothy Besley and Robin Burgess, "Political Agency, Government Responsiveness and the Role of the Press," *European Economic Review* 45 (2001): 629–640.

25 Philip Shabecoff, "The Environment Beat's Rocky Terrain," *Nieman Reports*, December 15, 2002. At http://niemanreports.org/articles/the-environment-beats-rocky-terrain.

26 Steven Clayman, Marc Elliott, John Heritage, and Megan Beckett, "A Watershed in White House Journalism: Explaining the

Post-1968 Rise of Aggressive Presidential News," *Political Communication* 27 (2010): 229–247, at p. 229.

27 Larry Sabato, *Feeding Frenzy: How Attack Journalism Has Transformed American Politics* (New York: Free Press, 1983), p. 31.

28 Sabato, *Feeding Frenzy*, p. 31.

29 Douglass Cater, *The Fourth Branch of Government* (Boston, MA: Houghton Mifflin, 1959), p. 107.

30 Cater, *The Fourth Branch of Government*, p. 111.

31 Katherine Fink and Michael Schudson, "The Rise of Contextual Journalism, 1950s–2000s," *Journalism: Theory, Practice, Criticism* 15, no. 1 (January 2014): 3–20.

32 Clayman, et. al. "A Watershed in White House Journalism," pp. 242–244.

33 Frank Esser and Andrea Umbricht, "The Evolution of Objective and Interpretative Journalism in the Western Press: Comparing Six News Systems Since the 1960s," *Journalism and Mass Communication Quarterly* 9, no. 2 (2014): 229–249.

34 Charles Hockett, "Chinese vs. English: An Exploration of the Whorfian Hypothesis," in Harry Hoijer, ed., *Language in Culture* (Chicago: University of Chicago Press, 1954) p. 122.

Chapter 10   Democracy as a Slow Government Movement

1 Dennis F. Thompson, "Representing Future Generations: Political Presentism and Democratic Trusteeship," *Critical Review of International Social and Political Philosophy* 13, no. 1 (March 2010): 17–37, at p. 17.

2 George Kateb, "The Moral Distinctiveness of Representative Democracy," in Kateb, *The Inner Ocean: Individualism and Democratic Culture* (Ithaca, NY: Cornell University Press, 1992), pp. 36–56.

3 Jerry Mashaw makes the distinction between political, managerial, and legal modes of accountability; I have added to his list public opinion or societal accountability. See Jerry L. Mashaw, "Bureaucracy, Democracy, and Judicial Review," in Robert F. Durant, ed. *Oxford Handbook of American Bureaucracy* (Oxford: Oxford University Press, 2010), pp. 569–589.

4 Danielle Kurtzleben, "Canada Reminds Us That American Elections Are Much Longer," National Public Radio, October 21, 2015. At https://www.npr.org/sections/itsallpolitics/2015/1 0/21/450238156/canadas-11-week-campaign-reminds-us-that-american-elections-are-much-longer.

5 Erica Morrell, "Public Comment Periods and Federal Environmental Impact Statements: Potentials and Pitfalls from the American Experience," *Michigan Journal of Sustainability* 1 (Fall 2013): 93–108, at p. 94.

6 Nadia Hilliard, *The Accountability State: US Federal Inspectors General and the Pursuit of Democratic Integrity* (Lawrence: University Press of Kansas, 2017).

7 James Madison, Debates, June 7, 1787. At http://avalon.law. yale.edu/18th_century/debates_607.asp.

8 The Federalist Papers: No. 63. At http://avalon.law.yale.edu/18th_ century/fed63.asp.

9 Cristiano Lima, "Obama Warns Against Impatience with 'Slowness of Democracy'", *Politico*, December 10, 2016. At politico.com/ story/2016/12/Obama-democracy-232462.

10 George Kateb, "The Moral Distinctiveness of Representative Democracy," in Kateb, *The Inner Ocean* (Ithaca, NY: Cornell University Press, 1992), pp. 36–56, at pp. 37, 40–41.

11 Farhad Manjoo, "Yesterday's News Today: Deep, Informed, Accurate and Inky," *New York Times*, March 7, 2018. The story can be found online at https://www.nytimes.com/2018/03/07/ technology/two-months-news-newspapers.html.

12 See http://nymag.com/daily/intelligencer/2017/02/andrew-sullivan-the-madness-of-king-donald.html.

Chapter 11   Second Thoughts: Schudson on Schudson

1 "The Unlovable Press: Conversations with Michael Schudson," *Journalism Studies* 18, no. 10 (2017): 1206–1342; special issue edited by Marcel Broersma and Chris Peters. The issue includes an introduction by Broersma and Peters, essays by C. W. Anderson, Rodney Benson, Martin Conboy, Lucas Graves, Brian McNair, Erik Neveu, Rasmus Kleis Nielsen, Christophe Raetzsch, and Silvio Waisbord.

2 Michael Schudson, "Symbols and Smokers: Advertising, Health Messages, and Public Policy," in Robert L. Rabin and Stephen D. Sugarman, eds., *Smoking Policy: Law, Politics, and Culture* (New York: Oxford University Press, 1993), pp. 208–225; and US Department of Health and Human Services, *Reducing Tobacco Use: A Report of the Surgeon General* (Atlanta, GA: US DHHS, Centers for Disease Control and Prevention, 2000).

3 Robert J. Samuelson, "Moving Toward the Mainstream," *Nieman Reports*, June 15, 2002.

4 Katherine Fink and Michael Schudson, "The Rise of Contextual Reporting, 1950s–2000s," *Journalism: Theory, Practice, Criticism*, 15, no. 1 (January 2014): 3–20.
5 Rodney Benson, *Shaping Immigration News: A French-American Comparison* (New York: Cambridge University Press, 2013).
6 Charles L. Briggs and Daniel C. Hallin, *Making Health Public: How News Coverage Is Remarking Media, Medicine, and Contemporary Life* (New York: Routledge, 2016).
7 Walter Lippmann, *Public Opinion* (New York: Free Press, 1997 [1922]) p. 183.
8 Lippmann, *Public Opinion*, pp. 240, 241.